THE

# Regal Rules
FOR *Girls*

# THE
# Regal Rules
## FOR Girls

How to find love,
a life—and maybe even
a lord—in London

# JERRAMY FINE

BERKLEY BOOKS,
NEW YORK

**BERKLEY BOOKS**
**Published By The Penguin Group**
**Penguin Group (USA) Inc.**
**375 Hudson Street, New York, New York 10014, USA**

Penguin Group (Canada), 90 Eglinton Avenue East, Suite 700, Toronto, Ontario M4P 2Y3, Canada (a division of Pearson Penguin Canada Inc.) • Penguin Books Ltd., 80 Strand, London WC2R 0RL, England • Penguin Group Ireland, 25 St. Stephen's Green, Dublin 2, Ireland (a division of Penguin Books Ltd.) • Penguin Group (Australia), 250 Camberwell Road, Camberwell, Victoria 3124, Australia (a division of Pearson Australia Group Pty. Ltd.) • Penguin Books India Pvt. Ltd., 11 Community Centre, Panchsheel Park, New Delhi—110 017, India • Penguin Group (NZ), 67 Apollo Drive, Rosedale, Auckland 0632, New Zealand (a division of Pearson New Zealand Ltd.) • Penguin Books (South Africa) (Pty.) Ltd., 24 Sturdee Avenue, Rosebank, Johannesburg 2196, South Africa

Penguin Books Ltd., Registered Offices: 80 Strand, London WC2R 0RL, England

This is an original publication of The Berkley Publishing Group.

Copyright © 2012 by Jerramy Fine.
A continuation of this copyright page appears on page 305.
Cover design by Sarah Oberrender.
Cover photos: woman with tea / Image Source / Getty Images.
Book design by Tiffany Estreicher.

PUBLISHING HISTORY
Berkley trade paperback edition / July 2012

Library of Congress Cataloging-in-Publication Data

Fine, Jerramy Sage, date.
The regal rules for girls / by Jerramy Fine.
p.    cm.
ISBN 978-0-425-24764-8
1. Etiquette for girls—Great Britain.
2. Dating (Social customs)—Great Britain.    I. Title.
BJ1857.G5F56    2012
395.1´44—dc23
2012005945

PRINTED IN THE UNITED STATES OF AMERICA

10  9  8  7  6  5  4  3  2  1

ALWAYS LEARNING

PEARSON

*If a stolid young Englishman is fortunate enough to*
*be introduced to an American woman, he is amazed*
*at her extraordinary vivacity, her electric quickness of*
*repartee, her inexhaustible store of curious catchwords.*
*He never really understands her, for her thoughts*
*flutter about with the sweet irresponsibility of*
*butterflies; but he is pleased and amused and feels as*
*if he were in an aviary.*
—OSCAR WILDE

# CONTENTS

# THE
# *Regal Rules*
### FOR *Girls*

*Don't follow your dreams; chase them.*

—Unknown

Everyone is constantly telling you how you have so much potential—that you could be a brilliant scientist or a successful attorney or some other esteemed profession that sounds incredibly taxing. But all you *really* want to do is fall in love with a hot British nobleman, live in his ancestral home, raise adorably polite children, work for a human rights charity, and breed dogs.

You are so not alone.

Come on—do you think Kate Middleton *really* wanted to be an art historian? The cynics among us can complain all they want, but there is no shame in admitting your dream and going after it if deep down that's what your heart desires. It doesn't make you silly and it certainly doesn't make you antifeminist. It's perfectly possible to have a brain *and* want a magical English life. So why not use that brain (and your heart) to go after it?

I'm not going to lie to you. Attaining this particular dream will be difficult. I mean, we can't all go to college with Prince William and one day marry the future King of England (although believe me, many of us have tried). But there are other ways to make your English fairy tale come true.

That's where this book comes in. Consider it your English fairy godmother. Every time you think that moving to England and chasing after titled men with irresistible accents is a harebrained thing to do, every time you're confused and upset about the hardships of expat life, and every time you're on the verge of giving up—this book will set you straight. It will help you approach what many deem to be an irrational, reckless goal—in a structured, logical way. Because you know what? I've been there. In the last ten years, I've cried too many tears, gone through too many work permits, lived in too many flats, squabbled with too many flatmates, drank far too many gin and tonics, and kissed way too many Hugh Grant look-alikes not to learn some valuable lessons along the way. This book will spare you the constant heartache and allow you to enjoy English society without fear of mindless American mishaps.

This is the British bible I never had but would have killed for. If I could go back in time, this is the book I *should* have devoured before catching my first dreamy flight to Heathrow. And now it is yours.

Read it.

Memorize it.

Use it.

And don't for one single second think that the life you dream of can't happen.

Because it can.

# ONE

# GETTING THERE

I'm sure when you envision yourself embarking upon your future English life, you picture yourself starting out in London. You picture a luxuriously bohemian existence in Notting Hill (perhaps opening a small bookshop); becoming a trendy publishing assistant like Bridget Jones; or applying to be the tea girl for the British prime minister (and ultimately seducing him). Your mind is swimming with all those quirky London flats, cobblestone streets, mansions with glowing windows, and adorably dithery rosy-cheeked Englishmen declaring love to the American girl of their dreams in the rain. (Or at a press conference, in the snow, or on Christmas Eve.)

Let's face it: Hugh Grant movies have a lot to answer for. Because although life in London *can* be as wonderful and as magical as Hollywood portrays, attaining it is not nearly that effortless. Getting to England is easy. Staying there, working there, and living there are other matters entirely. But I promise you, there is hope.

# Virgin Atlantic Is the Easy Part

I love Virgin Atlantic. Even though you're packed into a cheap economy seat, they try to make you feel like you're a first-class passenger. Movies on demand, late-night ice cream treats—flying with them is actually a pleasure.

But even if you plan on sleeping on the plane, try not to approach your flight like one giant slumber party. Sometimes, if you make an effort to wear nice clothes instead of a baseball cap and a comfy velour jumpsuit, Virgin will bump you to upper class—a part of the plane that has its own *bar*. (With actual stools.) And hey—if you're looking for a hot, successful, James Bond–type Englishman, you have a pretty good chance of meeting one here, so take it from me—wear your pearls, not your pajamas.

DON'T FORGET TO PACK:

- US-UK electrical adapters

- pocket-sized *London A–Z* street atlas (no other London map is worth having)

Still, as I mentioned before, crossing the Atlantic ocean is the easy part. *Getting* to England is easy. *Staying* is the hard part—especially if you want to do it legally. And considering you probably don't want to be an illegal UK immigrant working on the black market and in constant fear of deportation, I'm guessing you'll want to do it legally.

I know what you're thinking: The days of strict immigration rules are over. The Berlin Wall came down long ago and surely we're all free to live wherever we want. Right?

Wrong. Throwing your passport into the sea and becoming a free-moving citizen of the world is sadly not an option. (Believe me, I checked.)

Many are surprised by this because surely immigration rules aren't that strict in English-speaking countries. The truth is that they are *especially* strict in English-speaking countries. In fact, the country where immigration rules are the most rigorous is the country where English was actually invented.

But doesn't the UK government realize how much you *love* England? Don't they realize how much you *belong* on English soil? Don't they care that you understand the rules of hereditary titles or that you can name who is tenth in line to the throne? Aren't they even the *slightest* bit impressed that you can name the Commonwealth countries and quote Churchill and Shakespeare and Austen and Brontë until you go blue? What about the fact that you actually know the lyrics to "God Save the Queen"? Or the fact that you genuinely *like* milky tea, enjoy wearing tweed, and (vaguely) understand the rules of cricket?! Doesn't this count for *anything*?

Sadly not.

But don't give up or abandon your mission just because of a few bureaucratic barriers. *There are ways through this.* (And if it makes you feel any better, despite what the Statue of Liberty would lead many to believe, the United States is not that welcoming to Brits trying to live in America. So essentially, the "special US-UK relationship" is equally useless to all involved.)

I guess part of the reason the UK is so strict about who can and can't reside on their sacred isle is just that—they are actually a very, very small island. Let's not forget that the United Kingdom in total (including England, Wales, Scotland, and Northern Ireland) is roughly the size of Idaho. As much as the Brits might like to do so, they simply do not have the physical space to allow every Anglo-

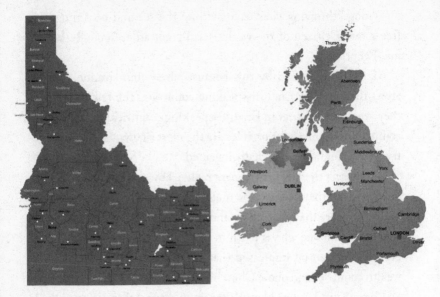

The state of Idaho compared to the United Kingdom

phile on the planet to live there permanently. So you just have to prove to them that you are an über-special, über-talented, über-dedicated, and über-deserving Anglophile.

## The Home Office

I'm assuming you already have a passport and I don't have to talk you through how to get one. Once that's out of the way, your exciting paperwork journey will begin with the *Home Office*. Google their site. Bookmark it. And get ready to refer to it more times than you care to remember.

The Home Office got its name in the same way "Homecoming"

got its name in America. The homecoming parade, homecoming dance, and homecoming bonfire are all celebrations to mark the fact that students, alumni, and town residents are coming "home" to watch one of the first football games of the season. This tradition is of course assuming that your high school is the center of the universe and you will never have another "home" quite like it. Similarly, the Home Office was named back when England considered itself to be the center of the universe, and no matter how much of the globe was conquered by the mighty British Empire, "home" would always be in England.

Despite being based in a well-mannered, orderly country, the service one receives from the Home Office is not particularly helpful. Or friendly. Or particularly efficient.* So don't expect American-style customer service, accountability, or transparency when dealing with them. Accept this early on and your frustration levels might drop a bit.

When it comes to getting yourself to the UK, I've narrowed it down to seven different options. Some are easier than others and some are more expensive than others—ultimately, you have to decide what is best for your circumstances and what you're hoping to achieve once you've landed on English shores.

## 1. A Student Visa

This option has the distinction of being both the easiest *and* the most expensive. It's the easiest because once you've been accepted

---

* Except when it comes to taking your money; you'll notice that these transactions usually happen at lightning speed.

to a British university to do your master's or your PhD (or even your BA)—the admissions boards at these schools don't care too much about your nationality. All they care about is that you have the academic standards required for their specific degree program. So if you're a bit brainy (and I'm sure you are), this is a superb way to further your education, study something you're passionate about, and get yourself to England on a student visa. Everyone wins: Your parents are proud, your mind gets challenged, and while you're there you just might get engaged to an earl.

There is a drawback to this option, and that's the price tag. Only a few years ago, college tuition was completely free in the UK. But in the last few years things have changed and now British students pay up to £9,000 per year for college (even for Oxford and Cambridge). Americans will have to pay "overseas tuition"—which is usually double the cost. But hey—this is still *a bargain* compared to the cost of most graduate degrees in the US.

What *can* be expensive is the *cost of living* in the UK, but luckily the benevolent US government offers reasonably priced loans to nearly all grad students who are US citizens. And those of you with an acceptable credit rating can borrow up to the *full cost* of attendance—including living and commuting costs—through the federal government's Grad PLUS program. On top of this, you're allowed to work in the UK up to twenty hours per week.

Worst case? You end up in just as much debt as all your American friends in law school or medical school. But *you* will have the added bonus of also living in England—which surely is worth every penny ten times over.

I'll be paying off my own student debt for the next thirty years—but my student loan is what made England possible for me and, in turn, opened up all kinds of opportunities that wouldn't have been there otherwise—so I don't regret it for a single, solitary second. I'm not encouraging you to rack up ten credit cards, but you should consider the fact that debt is not always a bad thing if it is the stepping stone that gets you what you want in life and leads you to where you want to be.

If you're serious about mixing with the British gentry, where you choose to study and what you choose to study is very, very important. I can't stress this enough.

My number one tip for degree-seekers abroad? Avoid London. I know it sounds heartbreaking to come all the way to England and not live smack-dab in its thriving, sparkling capital, but the truth is that most British students (especially ones destined to inherit titles and/or castles) don't go to university in London. If you want to meet American Ivy Leaguers and scores of European playboys, then a degree in London might suit you. Otherwise, steer clear.

**WHERE TO APPLY:**

- St. Andrews (the alma mater of Prince William and Kate Middleton)

- Oxford

- Cambridge (although considered much nerdier than Oxford)

- Edinburgh (full of Etonians!)

- Bristol

- Exeter

- Durham

- Sandhurst Military Academy (alma mater of Prince Harry and Prince William,* and yes, girls *can* apply)

FOR THOSE WITH MORE BEAUTY THAN BRAINS, TRY:

- The Royal Agricultural College

- Oxford Brookes

- University of the West of England

WHEN SELECTING A DEGREE, SAVVY GIRLS WILL CHOSE:

- History of Art

- Agriculture

- Geography

(Study as you intend to go on: think decorating your big stately home, making the most of your sprawling land, and traveling to exotic places on holiday.)

If you think any of these universities are out of your league, think again. Top-tier colleges in the US are actually far more selective and academically competitive. One of the biggest myths out there is you need to be a straight A student to get into "Oxbridge"† and this is categorically not true. British universities are more and

---

* Prince Harry attended Sandhurst instead of a traditional university. Prince William attended Sandhurst after graduating from St. Andrews—so he essentially has two undergraduate degrees.

† This is slang for Oxford or Cambridge.

more reliant on the higher tuition fees brought in by foreign students like you, and so my hunch is that they tend to be more lax when considering your application. Personally, I've yet to meet a single American student that was turned down by their top choice UK university. Perhaps I just hang out with über-intelligent people, or perhaps British universities just really, really like American students. Either way, if you're a decent student who works hard, don't let anyone discourage you from applying.

While three-year BA degrees are the norm in England, Scottish universities, like St. Andrews and Edinburgh, are particularly good options for American students because their undergraduate degrees last four years—giving you more time to strategically settle in your new homeland. Most UK master's degrees last one year only (half the time of the US equivalent)—which means you must move faster when it comes time to graduate and find a UK job and/or British husband.

The sad news is that after your degree is finished, your student visa is also finished, which (unless you're married to an earl by now) technically means you have to go back to America. But don't fret. You can either get another degree (albeit a bit pricey) or start working toward another one of my visa options.

## 2. An Ancestral Visa

The ancestral visa enables those with a grandmother or grandfather born in the UK to live in the UK for four years and eventually apply to stay permanently. Those living in the UK under this visa also have free access to the labor market upon entry. You have no idea how cool this is. Or how rare it is. It basically means you can work wherever you want and for whomever you want (be it Starbucks or Saatchi & Saatchi) without government restrictions. Of course you don't have recourse to public funds (the UK equivalent of welfare or food stamps), but that is par for the course with all visas.

I have to admit that I get really, really envious of people who have this option. So if you're eligible for it, thank the heavens for blessing you with such wonderful lineage and start applying!

## 3. A Religious Visa

This visa caters to those seeking to come to the UK to work as part of a bona fide religious organization (think ordained ministers, monks, nuns, missionaries, etc.). If you don't mind knocking on strangers' doors, passing out religious flyers, or committing to a life of celibacy and/or silence, then this is an excellent visa option. However, I would imagine that this visa is counterproductive when it comes to finding an aristocratic husband.

## 4. EU Citizenship

I'm warning you right now that this option is rather convoluted and may or may not require giving up your US passport in the process, as many EU countries don't allow dual citizenship. But I'm not one to judge your level of determination when it comes to making your English dream come true, so I might as well throw it out there.

Basically, if you are willing and able to live in another EU country (Portugal, for example) long enough to gain citizenship in that country, then as a EU citizen you are free to live and work in other EU member states—including the United Kingdom. Currently there are twenty-seven EU member states to choose from.

In almost all cases, there is a residence requirement of at least two years. Although I highly encourage you to do your own research (just Google various embassies for info), from what I can tell, Spain and Ireland have the fewest restrictions, along with some of the newer Eastern European countries that are trying to attract Western workers. Countries like Germany or Sweden are known for having tougher regulations.

Again, if you have a parent who was born in *any* of the twenty-seven EU countries, you may be eligible for citizenship, and once you've obtained it, you will be able to live and work in the UK! So if you're lucky enough to have family connections—*use* them!

## 5. Transferring to the UK with a US Company

Getting transferred to the UK office of the American company that you're already working for in the US is one of the easier options available. (This is because your American company handles all of the Home Office paperwork and expense.) Talk to your boss and HR manager and feel out what opportunities may be available to you in the UK—or even in the EU (see option 4). Believe it or not, not everyone is dying to drop everything and move overseas, and frequently companies are happy to have someone like you step forward for a transfer. No matter what, it can't hurt to ask. Nothing ventured, nothing gained.

If your current employer does not have an office overseas—find one that does. Get hired by them in America, give them at least eighteen months of your time, and then kindly request a transfer to London.

## 6. Getting Sponsored by a UK Company

This option is difficult, but it is *not* impossible. It involves coming to the UK (as a tourist* or student) and applying for jobs like a normal person. Except you're not a normal person—your life and your fantastic English future depend on getting sponsored by a UK company, so you'd better throw yourself into this job hunt 110 percent.

First create a CV (curriculum vitae) instead of a résumé. (This can be kind of fun because unlike American résumés, CVs can be two to three pages long and contain every single detail about your employment and educational history. No need to summarize your multitude of fabulous skills!) Of course you should send the CVs out to specific companies you'd really like to work for, but to be safe, I suggest blanketing the entire country with them. Don't forget to post your CV online, and to check job listings daily. (Monster, Jobsite.co.uk, and Guardian Online are good places to start.) Sending your CV to anyone and everyone you know that lives in London is also a good idea. Reach out to your university and sorority alumni; ask your parents if they have any British friends. It doesn't matter how tenuous the link—take any contacts that are proffered to you. Networking is a distinctly American strength— *use it.*

Buy yourself a few snappy suits because soon you'll start interviewing and eventually you'll get a job offer. (Trust me, it will happen. You're smart, charming, and well-presented. In fact, without even trying, you'll probably be the best-dressed person in the

---

* Do not get overly excited and tell the immigration officials that you hope to look for a permanent job or they might decide to send you right back to America on the next plane.

building. And since you're American, you'll also be refreshingly candid and eager. Employers will be falling over themselves to hire you.) The caveat to this, of course, is the tiny fact that you need a work permit. Employers are usually scared of sponsoring Americans because the Home Office makes it sound like a horrifically time-consuming and expensive process with tons of legal pitfalls that might get them into trouble. I'm not saying the sponsoring process is a joyride, but it's really not as bad as most UK employers tend to think.

Your employer must hold or obtain a sponsorship license, and once they have this it costs them nothing to apply for a visa on your behalf. The Home Office only doles out a set quota of sponsorship visas per month for entry-level jobs (with a minimum salary of £20k/year), but you and your potential employer are free to reapply every month until you get one.

A common myth is that your employer has to prove that you are better qualified for the job than anyone in the UK, EU, or Commonwealth. This is fundamentally not true. What your employer *does* have to prove is that you are better qualified for the job than anyone else in the world who's *applied for it*.

The Home Office requires your employer to advertise the position. Don't panic; placing one ad in an English-language EU newspaper with relatively low circulation counts as advertising. The ad should list every single qualification required for the position, making sure that you possess all of them. Every CV received in response to this ad must be examined with a fine-toothed comb, and if the candidate is missing even one of these qualifications he or she can be discounted. Eventually (hopefully) you will emerge as the most qualified candidate out of those who applied!

Some employers are nice enough to let you manage the above process for them. Others will insist on hiring an immigration lawyer to make sure it's done correctly. However, legal fees for this sort of thing can run between $3,000 and $5,000—which, as you can imagine, is quite an expensive gamble for an employer to take on behalf of a fresh-faced American they've only just met. If you can, offer to pay the legal fees (or have them deducted from your salary). This is a nice gesture which shows your dedication to the company.

The drawback of getting a sponsored work permit is if you decide to change jobs or leave the company, the visa is no longer valid and you must return to the US. With this option, it's hugely important to weigh up the strength of your love for England with your ultimate long-term career path.

## 7. Marriage to an Englishman (Preferably One with a Castle)

As this is the definitive goal anyway, you can probably stop reading this book. You're in love! Hurray! Not only have you found your English soul mate, but your geographical problems are solved and you can get started on redecorating that poor, neglected castle.

At one point, I wanted to live in the UK so badly that I briefly and very seriously considered marrying my gay best friend. Other than his sexual preference, he was pretty much everything I was looking for: cute, English, smart, funny. Not only would I have been able to live in England, the country of my dreams, I would have had a blast being his pretend wife! (Oh, the glamorous London parties we would go to! The gorgeously furnished flat we would share!) But this fantasy lasted approximately four days because more than several (rather humorless) people reminded me that it was against the law.

So that's the catch: Your marriage *must* be genuine. When it comes to this, the Home Office has eyes in the back of its head, and they *will* find out if you're faking a relationship just to live in the UK. At the end of the day, marrying someone just to stay in the country is illegal and can get you into very, very big trouble.

Still, that doesn't mean that finding true love and authentic marriage material in London is impossible. Not at all! The above is just a word of warning to prevent you from wasting a week contemplating marriage to your version of Rupert Everett.

Whether your fairy tale betrothal is the outcome of a whirlwind romance or something more enduring, any American girl marrying an Englishman must relinquish her passport to the Home Office for more than two months, provide multiple witness statements as to the validity of her relationship, and pay a fee of nearly $1,000. (What can I say? Home Office staffers aren't exactly die-hard romantics.)

Once approved, you can then apply for permanent UK residence (not citizenship—that comes even later). Still, with a little perseverance, more paperwork, more Home Office fees, and a stringent UK citizenship test, in due course the Queen of England can be your queen too. And I ask you: If that's not worth the bureaucratic hassle, what is?

## Note:

Please keep in mind that the Home Office changes their rules around all the time so please double-check with them or a reputable immigration lawyer before moving ahead with any of these options. (Also, beware of third party agencies that charge additional fees for handling your application—always apply directly to the Home Office or through a solicitor.)

Make sure to read the Home Office "guidance notes" carefully, and be certain you are reading the most recent version of these notes (they update about every eight weeks or so). I realize it's annoying to read through sixty-plus pages of fine print, but when it comes to something as important as your immigration status, you need to err on the side of paranoia. Make sure you convert dollars to pounds correctly, make sure you send in original bank statements (not copies), and make sure your bank account is in your name only (not a joint account with your parents).

I actually know someone whose visa application was rejected because he was "almost smiling" in his passport photo. It's true! I wish I could blame this on the sheer grumpiness of the Home Office—and partly I do. But apparently potential visa holders have been ordered not to look even remotely happy in their photos to avoid confusing the facial recognition scanners that are used at UK airports.

But it doesn't really matter—even if you look miserable in your application photo, the euphoria you feel when that UK visa is finally in your hands is probably akin to what you will feel upon the delivery of your firstborn child. So frown like you mean it.

USEFUL WEBSITES:

**Student Aid on the Web**—information from the US Department of Education on funding education beyond high school. http://studentaid.ed.gov/PORTALSWebApp/students/english/index.jsp

**The UK Border Agency at the Home Office**—where you can download all the forms and guidance. www.ukba.homeoffice.gov.uk/

**The UK Council of Student Affairs**—where you can find all the latest immigration info for international students. www.ukcisa.org.uk

SOME REPUTABLE UK LAW FIRMS:

**Xchanging Global Mobility Services** www.xchanging.com/XGMS/XGMSServices/Immigration.html

**CMS Cameron McKenna** www.cms-cmck.com/Immigration

**Fisher Meredith** www.fishermeredith.co.uk

**Dearson Winyard International** www.dwiglobal.com

# London Is the Best Place to Live on Earth. But Where Is the Best Place to Live in London?

If you're not going to come to the UK on a student visa, chances are that you will live in London. Without a shadow of a doubt, London is the most magical, the most beguiling, and the most charming city on the planet.

Whereas New York has the thrill of world finance and ground-breaking theater, Los Angeles boasts timeless Hollywood glamour, and Washington, DC, brings the buzz of power and politics—London has *all* of these things in one place. *Nowhere* else can you find economic, political, and artistic epicenters of such intense, global caliber rolled together into a single cosmopolitan capital.

Many compare London to Manhattan, but the truth is that London is far more elegant, the architecture is more beautiful, the streets are much cleaner, and the people are much calmer. I tend to get claustrophobic in New York, as you can walk for blocks among the towering scrapers without ever glimpsing the horizon. This is not the case in London. For almost 250 years, it was against the law to construct anything taller than St. Paul's Cathedral (365 feet high) so you can walk for miles without ever feeling trapped or overpowered by the city.

While New York is a true American melting pot, London is a collection of dozens upon dozens of distinct little villages. Every tube stop leads you to a new and extremely unique part of the capital, and there are so many secret alleyways and hidden courtyards, it's a city you can make your own like nowhere else. (A great way to get to know the city when you first arrive is to go on the Circle Line train and have a drink at every stop!)

On top of this, more than 30 percent of London is made up of sprawling parkland and manicured gardens—most of these were originally owned by the British royal family and used as their private hunting grounds before they were turned into public parks. With more than 5,550 acres of parks, ponds, forests, and flowers, London boasts more green space that any other major city in the world.

When I first arrived in London, I began walking everywhere, park after park, bridge after bridge, hardly knowing where I was going or where I had been. And hardly caring, because every single step seemed to feed my very soul.

On the second or third day, sometime in the early evening, I walked from the splashing fountains and giant lions of Trafalgar Square, past the famous door of 10 Downing Street, and then, suddenly, when I turned the corner, I was face-to-face with Big Ben. I found myself just standing there, gazing up into the rare blue sky at this magnificent clock tower that gleamed in the sunlight. I couldn't look away. Because all at once everything in my crazy heart and mind seemed to fall into place. Right in front of me was all the glory and sparkle that I knew my London life was going to be once I figured out how to grab on to it. After all those years of trying to escape everything around me, I suddenly felt something I'd never felt before: the desire to stay in one place forever.

## Finding a Flatshare

So you have your visa in your hands, you've said your good-byes to large American appliances, hot summers, and good water pressure, and you're ready to move to the city of your dreams.

Unless you're a secret billionaire, it's doubtful you will be able to afford to live somewhere in London on your own. Which means you must seek out a *flatshare*, which is an apartment shared by two to six people.

I know sharing houses with strangers is not commonly done in the US unless you're a starving student, but in London it's a pretty ordinary occurrence, even for well-bred, twenty-something professionals. Sharing is the best way to get a large, good-quality flat at an affordable price, and I promise you'll get over the weirdness of sharing a bathroom with people you don't know pretty quickly.

There are many ways to approach flat hunting. Finding a room through a friend of a friend of a friend is by far the best option, so start by asking people you know if they happen to know anyone with a room for rent and to spread the word that you are looking. Post your request on Facebook and send a mass email to everyone you can think of who might know somebody in London. Again, if applicable, contact your college and sorority alumni networks.

If you already have a British friend (or handful of friends) that you want to live with, it costs you nothing to go through a Realtor

(aka an *estate agent*) to help you find a furnished flat. (Rightmove
.co.uk is a good place to start.) But if you know no one, then grab
a notebook, grab your phone, and log onto all of the following:

www.flatshare.com

www.spareroom.co.uk

www.intolondon.com

www.roombuddies.com

www.uk.easyroommate.com

www.gumtree.com

www.london.craigslist.co.uk

www.loot.com

All of these websites are filled with flatshares seeking flatmates,
and most are categorized by price and location. (PS: Don't start
searching more than one month ahead of when you'd like to move,
as turnaround in London is quick.)

When I finished my master's degree, moved out of my awful
British dorm, and began to embark upon my first London flat
search, my specifications were simple: I was looking for a friendly,
English household full of young, non-married nobility begging to
adopt an American. But as time wore on and my search continued,
I was shocked to discover that even though London is the capital
of England, the city seemed to contain very few actual English
people. (And as for well-bred, English twenty-somethings desperate to take in a homeless American? Again, I blame my fantasies
on Hugh Grant movies.)

Something like a third of Londoners (and if you're there right now—this includes you) were not even born in the UK, and many London-based universities (especially the London School of Economics) are nothing more than hubs for wealthy foreign students, because most English students tend to go to college outside of the capital.

I'm not going to lie—meeting English people in London can be difficult. And because of this, it's all too easy to fall back on what you know. It's all too easy to start hanging out with other Americans and to start passing the time by drinking American beer in American-themed sports bars.

I don't know about you, but I was determined to do nothing of the sort. If I was going to be spending all my time with other Americans, I figured that I might as well give up on my English dream, go back to America, be near my American friends, get a nice American job, meet a nice American guy, and save myself and everyone else the transatlantic hassle.

As far as I'm concerned, coming to England and not mixing with English people is as pointless as a foreigner visiting America and not meeting any Americans. But if you choose wisely, your flatmates (even more than your workmates) will become some of your best friends in London, as well as introduce you to English social circles that an American would not otherwise encounter. So when it comes to selecting your accommodation—please believe me that your location (and hence your postcode) is absolutely crucial.

British postcodes are like US zip codes, except they also contain letters. London postcodes begin with N (for north), S (south), SW (southwest), and so on.

Among the London elite, it was once vehemently believed that the only truly suitable residential areas were located north of the

River Thames and south of Hyde Park—meaning that only a few neighborhoods (primarily SW1, SW3, SW7, and SW10) were deemed acceptable living quarters. Yet in the last few years, all these gorgeously grand town houses in Kensington, Chelsea, and Knightsbridge have been snapped up by Russian oligarchs and American bankers. (Some of these places go for as much as $10,000 per square foot!) So even though these historical dwellings are absolutely beautiful, today they are rarely owned or inhabited by English people.

This said, I suggest focusing on prospective flatshares in locations that are now quietly known as the *new* socially acceptable areas (meaning these are the natural stomping grounds for those upper middle-class Brits that speak in that sexy, expensively educated drawl that American girls like us find so irresistible):

Baron's Court—W14

Battersea—SW11

Clapham—SW4

Chiswick—W4

Fulham—SW6

Hammersmith—W6

Maida Vale—W9

Marylebone—W1

Putney—SW15

Wandsworth—SW18

If you can afford Notting Hill and Kensington (W11 and W8)—
go for it! Prime Minister David Cameron's family resides there,
and Freddie and Ella Windsor live there whenever they're in London, so you'd be in good company. (For those that don't know,
Lord Fredrick Windsor is thirty-eighth in the line of succession for
the British throne and a major pal of Prince William's. Lady Ga-
brielle Windsor is Freddie's sister and she is thirty-ninth in line.)

**PLACES TO AVOID AT ALL COSTS MAINLY
BECAUSE THEY CAN BE UGLY AND/OR UNSAFE:**

- The East End

- North London

The East End is considered edgy and trendy in a Guy Ritchie,
modern gangster sort of way (and it does contain the fabulous
Shoreditch House), but it's just too far away from the traditional
comforts of West London to be taken seriously by the "posh" English set.

As for North London (please note that the word "north" is usually said with a mix of fear and bewilderment), there is nothing
wrong with it—in fact, it's perfectly pleasant, and many Americans
choose to live there because it looks so neat and tidy. However,
North London is mainly full of other Americans, and is wholly
avoided by traditional, tweed-wearing Englishmen with ancestral
homes. There are a few exceptions to this: London Mayor Boris
Johnson lives in Islington and Peter Phillips (the Queen's oldest
grandson) once lived in Belsize Park. But as one floppy-haired
British boy once told me, "North London is a place one knows *of,*

but not a place one ever visits or fully comprehends." So I suggest you heed his advice.

Log onto flat search sites as early as you can in the morning (I'm talking inhumanly early—like 6 a.m.) and start calling asap. The demand for quality flats with normal flatmates is so high, many of the best ones are taken by 9 a.m. the same day.

When you find flatshares in the right areas within your budget (and it can happen!), you need to call them and make a viewing appointment. This is a chance for you to the view the flat and for the other flatmates to view you. As we used to say in my sorority rush days, it's a "mutual selection process." While on the phone, try to get as much information as possible about who lives there (guys? girls? nationalities? professions?), as you may decide it's not worth your time to go there in person. Due to the doors that can open in your London social life, I must stress that the quality of the people in a flatshare is even more important than the quality of the flat itself.

When out viewing flatshares, bring your *A–Z* with you. Many London streets have the same name (Kensington Place, Kensington Mews, Kensington Crescent, Kensington Gardens, Kensington Park Gardens), and it's easy to get lost if you don't have a map pinpointing the exact location.

Keep in mind that you will need to lower your expectations. Big-time. You're categorically not going to find American living standards at American prices, so push any thoughts along those lines out of your mind.

Before you open the door to a potential flat, expect the worst. Envision seventeenth-century plumbing and eighteenth-century electricity. Picture a bedroom three times smaller than your college dorm room but with ten times less storage space. Any London flat that exceeds this expectation even slightly is worth considering.

If your only problem with the flat is that the washing machine is in the kitchen, that the fridge is smaller than the TV, that there is no dryer for your clothes, that there is moldy carpet in the bathroom, that the bathtub has no shower attachment, or that the sinks have separate hot and cold water taps*—then put down an offer immediately. If the flat's inhabitants also happen to be polite, charming, and English—offer to pay double.

## Making Your Room Livable

When I moved into my UK student dorm room and later into my first grown-up London flat, I had no idea how and where to go about making either of them vaguely livable spaces.

The only way I can describe my London dorm is Orwellian mental institution meets abandoned crack house. (If you don't believe me, I have photo proof.) With its eerie green lighting, long dirty hallways, and exposed wiring, the place could easily have passed as a film set for a 1950s horror movie. The crazy part is that at the time I thought I was just incredibly unlucky and had simply been allotted the worst dorm in the country. But the longer I've lived in England, the more I've come to realize that this standard of student living is considered *normal*. A rite of passage, even. (One of my English friends told me how her dorm room was heated with a radiator that only worked if you deposited 10 pence every fifteen minutes.)

---

* This is actually disturbingly common. The simple pipe that allows one to mix both hot and cold water so you don't have to scald yourself every time you wash your hands or face is still very much considered a modern luxury. Double-paned windows are considered equally decadent.

And although my dorm room had been furnished with an electric kettle and a heated towel rack (both of which I had lived more than two decades without needing or missing), I had not been provided with a desk of any kind. I was, after all, just a student living in a student residence hall—why would I need one?

So I had to purchase, among many other things, a desk. I also needed to go shopping for things like clothes hangers, sheets, towels, and halogen lamps. And I needed a new radio and a curling iron because both of mine had short-circuited seconds after being exposed to the high-voltage UK electricity. If I had been in America, I would have just driven to Target. However, now that I was in London, I clearly didn't have a car, and more critically, England has nothing even vaguely similar to Target (much less Bed Bath & Beyond).

So here are the British alternatives:

### IKEA

You're probably already overly familiar with IKEA. They offer great quality, a great selection, and everything is very cheap and very stylish—but you pay for it in the end. You walk into IKEA and are tempted to buy everything in sight—until you get to the warehouse and realize you have to load the heavy items onto your cart by yourself, get them home (on the tube or via a very expensive taxi), and worst of all, put them all together piece by piece with things that you've never touched in your life, like hammers and screwdrivers. Instead of using a screwdriver, I tried to use a butter knife, and by the time I had (a) figured out where to buy a hammer and (b) finished hammering that stupid student desk together, I vowed that next time I would pay to have a desk custom made rather than go through the experience ever again. So when shopping at IKEA, take heed: buy only small items (like plants and posters) that you can carry home, or factor in the cost of a taxi, because IKEA charges a fortune to deliver. Also make sure you have a strong British boy at hand to help you construct any furniture that inevitably will emerge from the box in thirty-two pieces. (That said, it's probably good to have a strong British boy on hand for a variety reasons—not all IKEA-related . . .)

www.ikea.com/gb/en/

### Argos

Argos is like a really bad version of Sears. They have a catalogue and they have a weird "store" that you can go to where you point to things (like clock radios and curling irons) in their catalogue and the employees fetch them for you from some mysterious backroom. No browsing at Argos. But it's cheap, they have most basic items in stock, you can order online, and best of all—they deliver.

www.argos.co.uk

### John Lewis

John Lewis is a British institution. Everyone *loves* to love John Lewis. They are kind of like a JCPenney with an upscale Target in the basement. And weirdly, they are the only store in the UK that offers a wedding registry service. Most Americans find John Lewis (and their sister store, Peter Jones) to be a bit odd to begin with, but eventually they realize it really is the only affordable UK department store that can be counted on for quality. John Lewis recently launched a great new website *and* they deliver—so no expensive taxis required. www.johnlewis.com

# TWO

# LANGUAGE, MANNERS, AND BEHAVIOR

*(Because you don't have to marry a lord to act like a lady)*

## Parable #1

One of my best English friends (let's call her Hattie) is a girl from a meager yet loving English background. She studied art history at university, landed a job in one of London's oldest, most respectable auction houses, and now heads up all global marketing for one of the most famous companies in the world. She is good-looking, endearingly kind, incredibly well mannered, and clearly one smart cookie. Over the years, her working-class accent had vanished into something softer and convincingly appropriate for the upper-class clientele she worked with at the auction house, and when I first met her I was convinced she had been educated at one of England's prestigious girls boarding schools.

One Friday night, Hattie and I were barhopping on the King's

Road and we met, as we often did on that road, a lovely group of floppy-haired, rosy-cheeked, upper-class English boys. They all wore pink shirts (with sleeves rolled up just below the elbow, *never* above) and gold signet rings bearing their family's crest. They bought us round after round of gin and tonics, and before the night commenced, one of the boys (let's call him Edward) had asked Hattie to accompany him to dinner the next evening and to a hunt ball* in the countryside the following weekend. She was ecstatic (as I would have been!) and went shopping for a ball gown immediately.

When we met for cocktails the following week, I begged her to tell me every last detail. But as soon as I mentioned the ball, her face fell.

"What happened?" I asked.

"I was found out," she said sadly.

"What do you mean?" I asked.

"It was all going so well until the ball itself," she said. "I mean, our dinner the other night was amazing. Then Eddie and I drove out to Berkshire together . . . I met his sister and some more of his friends. They all seemed to like me."

"But then what?"

"I slipped."

"Slipped on what? Did you fall down?"

"No! Nothing like that . . . It happened at the ball. During the formal dinner. We were talking about Florence and . . . you know how much I *love* Italy because of the art . . . and I guess I just wasn't thinking because I accidentally . . . I accidentally . . . said *pasta* the wrong way."

---

* See "Formal Balls," page 152.

I stared at her incredulously. "You mean you pronounced it like an Italian instead of an English person?" (Believe it or not, in certain UK circles, there is nothing more uncouth than pronouncing foreign words correctly.*)

Hattie nodded. "They all stopped talking and just stared at me. And suddenly they *knew* I wasn't the person they thought I was. They *knew* that I wasn't like them. They *knew* I hadn't grown up like them. The rest of the night was really weird between us and I haven't heard from Eddie since."

It was a heartbreaking story. Through the misuse of a single word, Hattie's working-class roots had been revealed and Edward never called her back. It didn't matter that she made lots of money and dressed beautifully. It didn't matter that her manners were impeccable and that she had a career most girls would kill for. Hattie's linguistic faux pas gave the game away.

## Class Counts

*People think there's a rigid class system here,*
*but dukes have been known to marry chorus girls!*
*Some have even married Americans.*
—HRH Prince Philip, Duke of Edinburgh

The English are delightfully self-effacing, refined, and complex, but due to the class system that is engrained in the psyche of their

---

* For example, in England you must say chicken *fil-ET*, NOT chicken *fi-LAY* as the French word requires.

culture, if you don't play by the rules of the game, you can feel ostracized very quickly.

I had been in England less than a month when, through a mutual friend and an immense stroke of luck, I fell in with a dazzling English crowd. Their characters seemed to be taken straight from the pages of an Evelyn Waugh novel;* they were the *epitome* of the Bright Young Things; their parties even appeared in the back pages of *Tatler*!† And by some cosmic miracle, I (a farm girl from the backwaters of Colorado) was along for the ride.

My new English chums all looked and sounded and acted exactly the same. Same accents (upper-class), same fashion sense (the more faded and worn your clothes appeared, the more money you had), same skin (glowingly and annoyingly clear).

In their young minds, the past reigned superior: They liked *old* houses, *old* furniture, *old* wine, *old* money, *old* families. In fact, I noticed what seemed to be an almost fanatical preoccupation with genealogy. Unlike the American mind-set, which is primarily about what you can one day *become*, for these kids the focus seemed to be much more about what you had *been*.

I realize the very concept of a class system is hard for most Americans to grasp—after all, it's been drummed into our heads since birth that all people are created equal. But class pervades every single aspect of English life, so if you're going to immerse yourself in the country, you must be aware of the antediluvian mind-set that you're dealing with.

---

* *Vile Bodies* by Evelyn Waugh is a must, must read (and was later adapted for the 2003 film *Bright Young Things*). They are both too, too divine.

† *Tatler* is a glossy UK magazine depicting the glamorous lives and lifestyles of the upper class. Get yourself a subscription asap.

While American social divides are primarily about income, the English define themselves by a nonnegotiable set of qualities that have nothing to do with raw cash and everything to do with one's language, style, and manners. (Apparently there was a time when you could tell a man's rank, school, and era simply by how he folded his handkerchief.) If you pay close attention, you'll soon find that vocabulary, pronunciation, accents, etiquette, and clothes mean more than you ever dared to imagine . . .

## Watch What You Say

I'll never forget the day I found myself having real conversations with real English people that didn't involve buying a train ticket or saying thank you for my change. I was overjoyed, but at the same time, I quickly realized how innocent Americans are when it comes to language—how tiny, linguistic nuances in our conversations mean relatively nothing to us—but mean *everything* to the Brits. In a country where status is not determined by pure economics, I cannot overemphasize the importance the English place not only on what you say, but how you say it and with what accent—it is the most vital social signifier in the country.

An English aristocrat who speaks with upper-class pronunciation (clipped and plummy with lengthened vowels) and uses upper-class vocabulary, will *always* be considered and treated as an aristocrat, even if he is bankrupt, in prison, working in a factory, living in a mental institution, or living on welfare.

Conversely, a working-class Brit who has become a self-made billionaire, with private jets, expensive cars, and houses all around the world—will *always* be considered and treated like a member of the lower working class because he speaks with a working-class accent—no matter how much money he has and continues to make. Even if he changes his accent to something more neutral, one word of working-class terminology will automatically give him away—making it virtually impossible to ever truly shift his standing in the social order.

FOUR SURE SIGNS OF UK UPPER-CLASS SPEECH:

- The word "real" has two syllables.

- They pronounce "house" to rhyme with "mice."

- They say "gel" rather than "girl."

- "White wine" sounds like "wait wain."

If you want to know what an upper-class English accent sounds like, just watch any movie starring Hugh Grant or Rupert Everett and listen to their voices. This accent is what's known as "BBC English," "the Queen's English," "Oxford English," or "Upper Received Pronunciation" (URP) and is generally considered to be the *prestige* English accent, as it has been the accent of those with power, money, and influence since the early twentieth century.

(If you want to know what a working-class accent sounds like, watch something like *The Full Monty*, *Layer Cake*, or *Snatch*. There is nothing wrong with this accent—however, this book will focus primarily on the haunts and habits of those who speak with the URP.)

It's amazing, really—how the English can sum up another English person's entire family background (and hence their entire family's financial worth) simply by hearing how he or she pronounces certain words.

But the good news is that the Brits can't pigeonhole us Americans, because our accents give absolutely nothing away. Therefore, it doesn't matter in the slightest if you're from a poor background or a wealthy one; went to private school or public school; were raised by West Coast hippies or old money New Englanders.

Your accent—be it from the Bronx, Texas, Wisconsin, or a tiny mountain town in Colorado—doesn't come with any kind of class label, and the Brits cannot instantly judge you by the sound of it. They might be able to tell *where* in America you're from, but they can't tell anything about your socioeconomic background. To the Brits, you're a blank slate.

So as long as you maintain good manners, watch what you say, and conduct yourself with grace and poise, your neutral American accent will allow you to move through the upper echelons of English society at lightning speed. It's sad to say, but a working-class Brit would never be able to attain such rapid social mobility, because of the unbreakable accent barriers that still exist in the UK. But if you're American? London is your oyster.

Still, just because your US accent is neutral doesn't mean you can say whatever you like. Far from it. There are still plenty of rules to follow if you want to be warmly enveloped by the crème of British society.

DANGER WORDS (AKA WORDS TO AVOID AT ALL COSTS):

- "lounge," "front room," "living room," "couch," "settee" (I don't know why this particular part of the house causes such offense, but nevertheless, to avoid English shudders you should simply say "sitting room" or "sofa.")

- "serviette" (Always say "napkin." Even if you're in France. Don't ask me why.)

- "West End show" (Always say that you're going to the "theater.")

- "Pardon?" (Always say "I didn't catch that" or "Sorry?" or even just simply "What?")

- "Nice to meet you" or "Lovely to meet you" (Always say "How do you do?" This is a big one. Apparently, forgetting this rule when she first met the royal family nearly ruined things for Kate's mother, Carole Middleton.)

- "dessert" (Say "pudding"—even if it doesn't resemble anything close to pudding.)

## The T-word

Apparently saying the word "toilet" is just as jarring to an upper-class English ear as the f-word. In fact, I get the impression that they would actually prefer to hear the f-word. Bottom line? Never say "toilet." Ever. Not when referring to the bathroom; not even when referring to the porcelain bowl itself. You must say "loo": where is your loo; may I use your loo; the cat fell into the loo; he never remembers to put the loo seat down; I think we're out of loo paper. This rule is not optional; it's imperative.

Attempting to adopt English slang is another habit that is not going to do you any favors, since most slang has lower-class connotations. That said, you should avoid the following:

- "mate" (Just say "friend" like a normal person.)

- "cheers" (Unless you're making a toast, "thank you" will suffice.)

- ❧ "uni" (Just say "university"; don't say "college" or "school," as this means high school in the UK.)

- ❧ "tea" or "supper" when you really mean dinner (Just say "dinner.")

- ❧ "two month," "three pound," and so on (Forgetting to use plural forms is just poor grammar. Just because people in the North of England are doing it doesn't mean you should.)

KNOW THE DIFFERENCE:

There are literally *hundreds and hundreds* of words that are different in the UK: A cookie is a *biscuit*; a Band-Aid is a *plaster*, a shopping cart is a shopping *trolley*, and so on. I'm not going to list them all here as you will discover these as you go along and there are plenty of books supplying entire US-UK glossaries for you to peruse. Instead, I'm going to list a few important British words that you should be careful never to use incorrectly:

- ❧ "pants" (This means underwear in the UK; instead, say "trousers.")

- ❧ "suspenders" (This means garter belt in the UK; instead, say "braces.")

- ❧ "to snog" (This means "to kiss passionately," never to be confused with . . .)

- ❧ "to shag" (This means "to have sex with.")

LEARN:

- ❧ The value of exclamatory exaggeration: The choice of wine is simply . . . *heavenly, riveting, divine*; a broken toaster is . . . *ghastly, horrid, appalling*.

&#x25aa; The importance of understatement: Hurricanes? Middle Eastern conflicts? *So tiresome.* Traffic accident? Broken bone? *A bit
of a bother.* Hitler? *Not exactly the kindest person in the world.*

ENJOY USING:

&#x25aa; The elative letter D: *dazzling, devastating, divine.*

&#x25aa; The deflative letter B: *bloody, boring, beastly.* (The exception
here is *brilliant*—which cannot be overused.)

NOTE: When it comes to British conversation, discussing
money is to be avoided (just like in the US, talk of any kind about
how much things cost is considered vulgar); yet discussing the
weather is highly encouraged. In America, if you want to describe
someone as boring you might say, "She is the type of girl who en-
joys discussing the weather." In England, you are probably seen as
a boring person if you do *not* enjoy discussing the weather.

## Pronunciation

One of my favorite nail polish colors (the perfect 1950s red, perfect
for toenails) is called "Edinburgundy." Needless to say, it's a US
brand because I'm afraid the Scottish city of Edinburgh does not
rhyme with Pittsburgh. The correct pronunciation is *Ed-in-burra*—
to rhyme with Ventura.

But really, how are innocent Americans to know? The answer is
you're not. There are hundreds of similarly tricky words seemingly
designed purely to confuse anyone not born and raised in the UK.

Beauchamp is pronounced *Beach-um.*

Belvoir is pronounced *Beaver.*

Bohun is pronounced *Boon*.

Cholmondely is pronounced *Chumley*.

Colquhoun is pronounced *Cahoon*.

Featherstonehaugh is pronounced *Fanshaw*.

Marjoribanks is pronounced *Marchbanks*.

Epsom Derby is *Epsom DAR-by*.

Berkley Square is *BARK-ley* Square.

Leicester Square is *Lester* Square.

Gloucester Road is *GLOSS-ter* Road.

Gloucestershire is *GLOSS-ti-sher*.

Worcestershire sauce is *Wuss-ter-sher* sauce.

Magdalene College is *Maud-lin* College.

A clerk is a *clark*.

Strawberries are *straw-breeze*.

Sainsbury's (a UK grocery store) is pronounced *Sanes-breeze*.

Cadbury's chocolate is *Cad-breeze* chocolate.

Glasgow does not rhyme with "how" but with *go*.

And so on and so on. It would truly be impossible to list them all. I'm not asking you to fake an English accent; I'm just asking you to be vigilant about correct pronunciation. Keep your ears open and listen to how native speakers pronounce things before attempting them yourself.

# Your Accent

*American girls' voices are somewhat harsh . . . but after a time
one gets to love those pretty whirlwinds in petticoats that
sweep so recklessly through English society.*
—Oscar Wilde

This is one of the biggest pieces of advice I can give you: do *not* attempt to fake an English accent. It just sounds silly and it will *not* endear you to the Brits. I can *always* spot an American who has lived in London for less than a month yet is trying to sound as if she's lived here her whole life. I'm telling you, not only is it glaringly obvious, it's extremely embarrassing for everyone around you. And this is mainly due to the simple fact that a proper English accent is extremely hard to replicate correctly.

While it is correct UK English to pronounce "bath" so that it rhymes with "sloth," most Americans tend to overdo this particular vowel sound, and more often than not, they overdo it in the wrong way. For example, Americans attempting to fake a "posh" English accent usually pronounce, "relax" so that it rhymes with "fox," or "understand" so that it rhymes with "pond." (Both would be incorrect. And both would sound ridiculous.)

Since words like "cancer" and "dancer" do not rhyme in the UK like they do in America, guessing which sound to use for which words can be a minefield. So unless you're Gwyneth Paltrow or Anne Hathaway and have endless Hollywood voice coaches at your disposal, *don't do it.*

Instead, soften your American accent a bit—lower the volume (then lower it again). In England, speaking loudly is a sure sign of ill breeding, and in fact, the best compliment you can possibly receive from a Brit is that you "seem *quiet* for an American."

Tone down the nasal, whiney sounds (we all have them), and work on pronouncing those pesky t's. (It's water; not *waa-der*. It's tomato; not *toma-doe*.) If you do these simple things, you'll be surprised at how many *compliments* you'll receive on your gentle American accent. Some will call it sweet. Some will even call it sexy! Don't try to be or sound like something you're not; instead make the most of what you have.

REQUIRED VIEWING:

### My Fair Lady

This happens to be my favorite movie of all time. It's based on George Bernard Shaw's play *Pygmalion* and is the story of an impoverished young girl named Eliza Doolittle (played by Audrey Hepburn) who sells flowers on the dirty streets of London. When a wealthy linguistic professor named Henry Higgins hears her piercingly crass working-class accent (sounds "like chickens cackling in barn," he says, "I'd rather hear a choir singing flat"), he makes a bet with a friend that a few weeks of speech coaching is all it will take to pass off this "guttersnipe" as a duchess. Eliza agrees to participate in this wager, and by the end of the movie everyone at the Embassy Ball is convinced that she is of royal blood. And Henry falls in love with her of course. But the most important part is that everyone thinks she's royal just because her accent changed, when only months ago she was a common ruffian living on the streets.

Excessive childhood viewings of *My Fair Lady* actually proved to be an invaluable education for me when it came to understanding the intricacies of the English class system, and the knowledge I gleaned from it served me well when I arrived in London. I advise you to watch it and learn. (And I promise, by the end of the movie, you'll find yourself happily humming the soundtrack.)

RECOMMENDED READING:

*Watching the English* by **Kate Fox**

This endlessly entertaining book observes the British with a sharp, anthropological eye, as if they were animals in the wild. Breaking down all facets of British life within the strict UK class structure, the author examines mundane British activities like shopping, gardening, and breakfast and the subtle differences found amid the upper class, middle upper class, upper middle class, middle middle class, lower middle, upper lower, middle lower, and so on. Truly eye-opening stuff. You will never look at the Brits the same again.

# Parable #2

My friend Matilda (known as Tilly) is very posh. And very picky. At least when it comes to men. For a while she was the only girl in London who seemed to be dating more than I was—and eventually she eclipsed my efforts completely. Still, I'll never forget the day she told me she had found "the one."

"His Internet profile is perfect," she gushed in her hyper–blue blood voice. "He's witty, he's clever, he's taller than me, he plays rugby, he skis, he sails, and he speaks French, German, *and* Italian! We're going to dinner tomorrow night!" She was practically squealing with delight.

The next day, when I called to see if the two of them were engaged, she sounded absolutely crestfallen.

"Was he not good-looking in real life?" I asked.

"He was gorgeous!" she answered, "I wanted to rip his clothes off."

"So what's the catch?"

"I'll tell you what the catch is," she said bitterly. "The boy does not hold his knife correctly. I sat through our entire meal thinking how I could never bring him home to my parents. They'd kill me if I married someone with even slightly deficient KFS skills."

"KFS skills?"

"Knife, fork, spoon. It's army talk. KFS skills are very important to my family. Have been for generations. And rightly so. No, it's probably for the best that I break things off with Charlie right now. He *is* gorgeous . . . but it never would have worked."

The lesson? In England, table manners are important. Really important. It doesn't matter how cute or smart you are—what you do with your cutlery on the first date can literally make or break a relationship.

# Manners

*Thirty years ago, in England as well as on the Continent,*
*the American woman was looked upon as a strange*
*and abnormal creature, with habits and manners*
*somewhere between a savage and a chorus girl.*
—LADY RANDOLPH CHURCHILL, 1910

Rightly or wrongly, if there is one thing the English have a reputation for, it's manners. It's important to remember that manners are not about being superior to others, but about making those around you feel comfortable. Whether it's dinner with your British boss, lunch at an English friend's house, or a date with the Englishman of your dreams, simple etiquette skills give you the confidence to handle any situation and put those around you at ease. Manners are not only enabling, they are disarming—and far from being something antiquated that is no longer relevant, they are a vital part of London life.

When I moved to England at the age of twenty-two to pursue my master's degree (and to pursue a noble English husband), I already knew (or thought I knew) the basics of English etiquette, mainly because I'd spent so many of my teenage years devouring books on American etiquette. However, whereas Emily Post is the goddess of US manners, she seemed to know relatively little about what I was encountering at UK dinner parties.

To me, the list of unwritten English rules seemed endless, and the smallest blunders on my part would occasionally cause a flurry of barely concealed shudders among my new friends. English etiquette, especially among the upper-class characters I was mixing with, was a minefield—and I wanted to get it right.

As part of my self-taught assimilation course, I decided to memorize *Debrett's Guide to Etiquette and Modern Manners*. Debrett's was founded in 1769 (before the USA even formally existed) and is really the only true authority on proper English behavior. I read it cover to cover, determined to encapsulate all of its wise teachings.

The more I read, the more I realized how little I knew. There were tons of English rules that I'd never heard of, and I have to say, when I first read about them, their arcane absurdity astounded me. From what I could tell, dozens of invisible, nonfunctional rules existed purely to ostracize those that knew them from those that didn't. (And to allow those in the know to tell terribly amusing anecdotes about those who weren't.)

For example, port must always be passed clockwise. You don't talk about it. It just happens. And if I hadn't happened to read about this universal beverage traffic law the night before I attended a glamorous British dinner party, the port's journey would have stopped with me, and everyone would have enjoyed being silently aghast at my American ignorance and talked excitedly about the incident among themselves for weeks to come.

Then there's the monstrous challenge of correctly eating something as simple as peas. Little did I know that the correct way to consume peas is to squash them on top of your fork! By this I mean you must use your knife (held in your right hand) to smash the peas violently against the back of your fork (which you are holding in your left hand with the prongs facing down) until they are sufficiently mushy and secure, after which it is safe to bring the fork to your mouth (prongs still facing down). No piercing of peas is permitted; no scooping of peas is permitted. And *under no circumstances* are you to turn the fork over and push the peas onto the inside of the fork with your knife.

So *please* study your etiquette.

Because unless you know the rules, how can you break them?

> *Never be ashamed to acquire the smallest grace*
> *by study and practice.*
> —THE LADY'S BOOK OF LONDON MANNERS, 1890

## Continental Dining

I'm not sure Americans realize how silly our table manners look to the rest of Europe. We cut a piece of steak with the knife in our right hand, put the knife down, pick up the fork in our right hand, spear the piece of steak, and then bring it to our mouth. Then we switch the fork to our left hand, pick up the knife and cut another piece of steak. There's a lot of zigzagging and hand switching going on for every single bite. If you do this in the UK, it's social suicide.

I'm telling you, the Brits will look at you like you're some kind of swamp creature. And if a well-bred British boy sees you do this, there is absolutely no way he is bringing you home to meet his aristocratic mother.

So *please*, take my advice and master the art of continental dining. It is by far the most graceful way of eating, but it does take practice.

- Hold your fork in your left hand (prongs facing down).

- Hold your knife in your right hand.

- Handles should be held tucked into the palm, with the index finger resting along the top edge of each handle.

- Cut a small piece of food, then, using your knife, press it firmly onto the fork (which is still facing down) and bring the fork (still facing down) directly to your mouth. The knife remains in your right hand and is held low to the plate between cuts.

- Never place the knife or fork back onto the table.

- Never hold your knife like a pen or your fork like shovel. (Ever.) Beware that in certain English circles they will refer to a person with poor table manners as "HKLP" (Holds Knife Like Pen).

- Never eat off the knife.

- Never cut food with the side of your fork.

- If you want to sip some wine, use your napkin, finish telling a very long story, or take a break of any kind, you must place the knife and fork in the resting position. (See illustration below.)

- If your food does not require a knife (salad, cake, etc), it's okay to have the fork in your right hand, prongs facing up.

- Your soup spoon is held in your right hand. Soup should be scooped up by tilting the spoon away from you, and to reach the last drops, the bowl should be tilted away from you.

- When you have finished eating, place your cutlery side by side, with handles facing five or six o'clock. (See illustration.)

I used to tell myself that it really didn't matter which fork I used for which course as long as I made an effort to make the people I spoke to at dinner feel valued. But I soon learned that this is nothing but American silliness. In reality, if the Brits see you do something incorrectly, they wouldn't dream of saying anything (they

Left: resting position
Right: finished position

are, after all, the "very pineapple of politeness"*), but rest assured they will make a quiet mental note against your character. So please, please, pay attention to the following:

PLACE SETTINGS:

- Place your napkin in your lap as soon as you sit down.

- When faced with a dazzling array of cutlery, the golden rule is start on the outside and work your way in.

- If you're nervous and can't remember which fork to use, wait to see what others do first.

- Your bread plate is on your *left*. Your wine and water glasses are on your *right*.

- Put butter onto your bread plate—never directly onto the bread. Break off a small chunk of bread and butter each chunk separately as you eat. (Never slice the bread in half and butter the entire slice.)

- If you must leave the table in the middle of the meal, leave your napkin on your chair.

- At the end of the meal, leave your napkin scrunched (never folded) on the table.

---

* This line is attributed to London playwright R. B. Sheridan—and I think it's one of the best sayings ever.

DINING DOS AND DON'TS:

- DO sit up straight.

- DO close the menu once you've decided.

- DO wait for everyone at the table to be served before eating. Even if the hostess says, "Please begin"—it's good manners to wait. (If you are seated at a large banquet, it's fine to begin eating once guests on either side of you have their food.)

- DO learn to eat pizza, burgers, and French fries with a knife and fork. (I'm serious. The Brits actually do this.)

- DO fill others' glasses before filling your own.

- DO pass the salt and pepper together.

- DO ask for a fork if you can't use chopsticks.

- DON'T express distaste for the food if others are enjoying it.

- DON'T order something if it's messy or you're not sure how to eat it (fish with bones, spaghetti, etc).

- DON'T pick up a canapé unless you can consume it in a single mouthful.

- DON'T touch up your lipstick or powder your nose at the table.

- DON'T leave your evening bag or phone on the table (though DO switch your phone to silent).

- DON'T ask for a "doggie bag"—taking leftovers home just doesn't happen.

# Afternoon Tea

*You must not refuse cups of teas under the following
circumstances: if the weather is hot; if the weather is cold;
if you are tired; if anybody thinks you are tired; before you
go out; if you are out; if you have just returned home;
if you feel like it; if you don't feel like it;
if you have not had tea for some time;
if you have just had a cup.*
—George Mikes

In England, tea has endless magical qualities and is genuinely believed to solve everything. Your boyfriend breaks up with you? Tea.
Come down with the flu? Tea. Terrorist attack on the London Underground? Tea. (Americans go to red alert, the Brits put the kettle
on.) When in doubt, put the kettle on.

When I first began working in London, it was the middle of a
rare heat wave and I was eternally puzzled that my new British coworkers would offer me a cup of tea every single afternoon even if
it was eighty degrees outside. (When I brought in a box of Popsi-
cles* to share, everyone looked at me like I was nuts.)

During a vacation to Antigua, where it was nearly a hundred
degrees outside, I watched in amazement as all the Brits promptly
left the blazing sun of the beach at 4 p.m. to go inside and enjoy a
scalding cup of tea.

While I believe tea will warm you if you are cold, I have yet to
convert to the English belief that tea will cool you if you are hot,

---

* aka "ice lollies."

cheer you if you are depressed, or calm you if you are nervous. (In the UK, tea seemingly has the miraculous ability to be both a sedative and a stimulant.) Yet when I stopped viewing tea as just a drink and started seeing it as it really is—a *pastime*—I began to enjoy it immensely.

Still, I'll never forget when one of my cute British flatmates told me that I made the worst cup of tea he'd ever tasted. I was flabbergasted at this insult. I mean really, tea is tea—right? Apparently not. All Americans know that it's perfectly possible to have a bad cup of coffee, and likewise, if you don't know what you're doing, it's quite easy to make a bad cup of tea. So practice your technique—because if there is one way to a cute British guy's heart, it is the perfect cup of tea.

RULES FOR AFTERNOON TEA:

- Always say "*afternoon* tea," NOT "high tea." High tea is a working-class evening meal.

- Always use a teapot filled with brewed tea rather than individual tea bags.

- When pouring tea, the spout faces the pourer.

- Unless you are using antique bone china that might

shatter at the splash of hot liquid, tea is poured *before* adding milk. This also allows you to judge the tea's strength.

- The working classes tend to drink strong tea with lots of milk and even more sugar (this is often referred to as "builder's tea"), but I advise you to learn to love the upper-class version, which is weak, unsweetened Earl Grey with a dash of milk.

- No lemon. No honey. These are purely American accoutrements and will not be found on tea trays anywhere in England.

- If you must have sugar, anything more than half a spoonful will be deemed suspect.

- When stirring your tea, do not clank the sides or swirl the tea around. Instead, stir the tea gently in a twelve-o'clock-to-six-o'clock motion.

- When finished, place the spoon on your saucer, never on the table, and never leave it in your cup. (I actually received a letter of complaint from an Englishwoman who was appalled at the illustration on the hardcover of my memoir, which depicts the ghastly crime of a spoon sitting in a teacup and not on the saucer where it belonged.)

- If seated at a table, lift the tea cup from its saucer. If standing or sitting on a sofa, hold the saucer as well as the cup.

- Teacups are not coffee mugs, so do not cradle them with both hands. Instead, hold the handle with your fingers and thumb.

- Try not to lift your little finger, but if you must do this to balance the weight of the cup, then it is perfectly acceptable to do so.

- Sip tea gently. Do not slurp.

- Finger sandwiches are meant to be consumed with your fingers.

- Scones should be sliced in half horizontally and then topped with jam and clotted cream.

- When you pronounce "scone" it should rhyme with *John*, NOT with "bone."

- Clotted cream is like a cross between butter and ice cream— sweet, thick, and dreamy. There is a regional debate over whether cream or jam is spread first on a scone (in Devon, they believe cream comes first; in Cornwall, they believe jam comes first). As an American, this is one case where you can do what you like.

- Scones are not donuts. Please don't dunk them in your tea.

BEST AFTERNOON TEAS IN LONDON:

I highly recommend that you discover this decadent and delicious English pastime for yourself. My favorite afternoon teas are listed below:

### The Orangery at Kensington Palace

Set beside Kensington Palace, and along the meticulously mani-cured Kensington Gardens, this is a refreshingly affordable teahouse for girls seeking royal refuge and refueling. The Orangery itself, designed for Queen Anne in the eighteenth century, is a glass build-ing with magnificent Corinthian columns. Tea is served à la carte (which is great for those days when you're not in the mood for sandwiches *and* scones *and* cake). That said, piles of scones and a wide assortment of traditional cakes are tiered on a grand central table, so you can peruse your options before ordering. In the summer you can sit out on the terrace and ponder the regal view. The Orangery does not take reservations, but it's worth the wait. www.hrp.org.uk/ kensingtonpalace/Foodanddrink/Orangery.aspx

### The Soho Hotel

Another reasonably priced tea option, this hotel is one of the most glamorous destinations in the bustling heart of London. Afternoon tea can be taken in the hotel's sumptuous Drawing Room or in the Library—both overflowing with plump cushions, velvet sofas, and to-die-for drapes. I held my London "hen" party here (that's what they call bachelorette parties), and it was the perfect place for ten girls dressed in mandatory pearls and twinsets (I couldn't have dreamed of a better dress code) to scoff pink champagne, lemon drizzle cake, and strawberry tarts before heading to the Roller Disco à la Kate Middleton.* Call ahead to reserve. www .firmdale.com/london/the-soho-hotel/afternoon-tea

### Claridge's

When Claridge's first opened back in 1812, it quickly gained a worldwide reputation among aristocracy as the *only* place to stay when one was visiting the British capital. During the aftermath of World War I, many aristocrats were forced to sell their splendid London houses and move into Claridge's on a permanent basis. (Believe it or not, without the expense of maintaining a large

---

* Kate famously attended a 1980s-themed roller-skating disco in aid of Oxford's Children Hospital.

household staff, to many, this arrangement was actually *cheaper*.) And during World War II, when many of Europe's royal families were dramatically exiled from their countries and palaces, once again dozens of noble families sought permanent refuge at this luxurious five-star hotel. So, basically, if you're of royal blood and have nowhere to go—Claridge's is the place for you. (In retrospect, instead of enduring the trauma of my English dorm for a single minute, I should have headed straight to Claridge's and announced that I was a victim of royal exile.) There is a famous saying that goes, "To arrive at Claridge's is to have arrived." And when you walk through the opulent, art deco lobby of this historic hotel, you'll know why. Afternoon tea is pricey, but it is "all you can eat" so feel free to ask for extra trays of scones. Reservations are essential. www.claridges.co.uk/

## Thank-You Notes

Handwritten letters are a dying art, and England is one of the last bastions where the art of correspondence still thrives. After all, it wasn't that long ago that mail was delivered regularly four times a day and Londoners thought nothing of posting a letter in the morning for a friend to read at lunchtime! The Royal Mail really is one of the glories of the nation. You can walk into a UK drugstore (or "chemist") and ask for a popular brand of shampoo and be told sorry it's on order and will take ten days; dry cleaning can take anything from three weeks to three years—but first class letters always miraculously arrive within twenty-four hours of posting.

Yes, sending an email is easier. But because we are living in a world where even our parents are on Facebook, handwritten correspondence is more important (and more meaningful) than ever before. Princess Diana was known for sending thank-you notes for even the smallest of deeds and doing it almost immediately. It can't hurt to emulate this royal icon for a variety of reasons (fashion and philanthropy at the forefront), but getting into her habit of writing thank-you notes is a good place to start. It takes no time at all (you can start and finish a note while your tea is brewing), and even less if you have the proper writing equipment.

- Invest in a box of luxury, watermarked stationery (Crane and Smythson are my favorites); if you can afford to, get it personalized with your address (but never your name).
  www.crane.com
  www.smythson.com

- Remember that you must always say "writing paper," never "notepaper."

- Use a nice, pretty pen (anything that is not a leaky ballpoint will do).

- Write your thank-you note as soon as possible after receiving the gift/hospitality.

- Your note should be personal, sincere, warm, witty, and to the point.

- Thank-you notes should not sound overly formal; instead write as if you're speaking to the recipient.

- Place a first class stamp of the Queen in the corner of the envelope, and walk it to the nearest red postbox. (If done correctly, you'll feel like a character in a Jane Austen novel.)

## Kissing Confusion

It was my junior year in college when I first arrived on British shores. After being housed in a giant flat with nine other American girls, I was desperate to make it through the mandatory "cultural assimilation" week that my university had organized. I couldn't wait to escape the lectures on which way to look when crossing the street and start my full-time internship at the Houses of Parliament.

It was during this time that I met an English boy my age named Rupert. Rupert sat at the desk across from me, brought me cups of tea (whether I wanted them or not), and teased me endlessly about my royal obsession. One night we went out drinking with the other parliamentary interns, and afterward Rupert walked me to the tube station like a true gentlemen. As we said good-bye, he leaned in and *kissed me* on both cheeks. I was utterly confused. Did he *like* me? Did he "like me" like me? And if not, why the kisses?

Then Rupert introduced me to his friends (those Bright Young Things that I was telling about), and I realized that everyone in England kissed everyone on both cheeks when they said hello and good-bye—and that romance had nothing to do with any of it. Girls cheek-kissed their girlfriends; girls cheek-kissed their guy friends; guys cheek-kissed their girlfriends—the only time hands were shaken was when guys greeted other guys. Although this pervasive cheek-kissing movement originated in continental Europe, it is now common practice in the UK. So here's what you need to know:

RULES FOR CHEEK-KISSING:

- Do not cheek-kiss anyone you've just met; a handshake will suffice. (Though you may find that a cheek-kiss seems more natural when you say good-bye.)

- Do not cheek-kiss anyone that you work with in a professional context. (Rupert and I were more drinking buddies than professional colleagues, which is why it worked in this instance.)

- Do not attempt to cheek-kiss anyone who is wearing a wide-brimmed hat (or if *you* are wearing a wide-brimmed hat).

- Put an arm lightly around the other person's shoulder and lean in slightly. Usually the right cheek gets kissed first, but this changes depending on the person (and their nationality).

- Air kisses are fine, but there should be no sound effects.

- If you need to say good-bye to a large group, there is no need to cheek-kiss every single one of them (waving or blowing a kiss to the group is more appropriate).

- Hugs are rare in the UK for anyone other than close family, so try to restrain your American tendencies.

RECOMMENDED READING:

*Debrett's Etiquette for Girls*
The one and only British authority on all matters of modern etiquette, taste, and achievement. This fantastic guide is full of great advice including tips for entertaining at home and getting ahead at work.

# THREE

# LONDON STYLE

*If you consider that when you are far away from home
and surrounded by strangers, you are judged entirely
on the strength of your external appearance, perhaps
you will realize the importance of being flawlessly
well-dressed wherever you travel.*

—GENEVIEVE ANTOINE DARIAUX

Let's face it: Nothing screams American more than sneakers and baseball caps. As we all know, there's absolutely nothing wrong with being American—but drawing attention to the more negative American stereotypes is not going to help your cause.

When I first moved to London, I couldn't believe how much women seemed to dress up just to go grocery shopping on a Saturday afternoon. What I didn't quite comprehend was that these women were not dressed up, they just don't dress down. European cities have much stricter sartorial standards than American cities. You can't come to London and dress as if you are lounging about in your LA apartment—it just doesn't work like that.

Sitting on the tube, I can always tell who the tourists are because they dress for a day in London as if they are going on a hiking expedition through the Rocky Mountains—sneakers, fanny packs, baseball caps, windbreakers, etc. Half the time I'm surprised they don't have walking sticks. These people just don't seem to comprehend the concept of "city attire."

In London, you don't step from your home to your car and from your car to your destination. Living in London means taking public transportation and walking around on real streets. It means fantastic people watching, but it also means understanding that those same people are watching you!

This doesn't mean you have to buy a whole new wardrobe or start dressing like a catwalk model in order to survive in England's capital city. Far from it. All it means is that you need to think twice before leaving your flat.

### HOW TO DRESS FOR LONDON LIVING:

- Ignore fashion trends and stick with the classics. (Skinny jeans belong on Kate Moss—not Kate Middleton.)

- Learn to love cashmere and tweed.

- Buy one pair of nice boots that you can wear with jeans or skirts.

- Don't be afraid to wear skirts* for any and all occasions—even for casual outings to the park.

---

* Unless you have zero hips, slim thighs, and a tiny bottom (aka "bum")—and let's face it—most of us don't—your skirt hem should hit *directly below your knee*. Not only is this length classy and feminine, it draws attention to the slimmest part of your leg. If the hem is shorter or longer than this, you are in danger of making your thighs/calves look like tree trunks.

- Invest in a pea coat that will last you a decade and a cocktail dress that will last a lifetime.

- Wear pearls. They are simple, elegant, and go with everything. And compared to other jewelry, they are relatively inexpensive. Invest in a pair of studs and wear them everywhere.

- Carry a timeless, versatile handbag. Longchamp is a catch-all classic that is reasonably priced until you can afford Mulberry or similar.

- Heels? As often as you can. (See "City Shoes.")

- When in doubt, less is more. (Coco Chanel famously suggested that a woman should remove at least one accessory before leaving the house.)

- If you're unsure of the dress code, ask.

- Remember: classy trumps cool every single time.

CITY SHOES

- I've always believed a girl should keep her heels, head, and standards high. But heels shouldn't be so ridiculously high that you look like a cartoon, and ultimately, you want to be able to walk! (You literally should be able to walk comfortably in your heels for a full mile—which is the minimum daily walk for most Londoners.) Two and a half inches is just about right; anything higher is perilously close to porn star territory.

- London's ancient cobblestones can be quite aggressive on both your shoes and your body—so when it comes to high heels, make sure you have a good cobbler and a good chiropractor close at hand! I'm a stickler for fashion, but it's not a sign of weakness to admit that there are times when cute ballet flats or comfy leather riding boots might be more appropriate.

WHAT NOT TO WEAR (UNLESS YOU'RE AT THE GYM):

- your sorority letters
- baseball caps
- sweatpants
- running shoes
- windbreakers
- anything supporting a US football, basketball, or baseball team

# Cambridge Chic

*Be loyal to the royal within you.*
—UNKNOWN

You absolutely cannot go wrong if you try to emulate the eternally fabulous Duchess of Cambridge. Kate is wonderful: always poised, always confident, and always classy. Not only will she be the first British queen with a university degree, but she has shown that no matter what your background may be, if you conduct yourself with the grace of a princess, you have every right to move in royal circles. Kate's very presence on the balcony of Buckingham Palace has shown ordinary women (women who value ideals based on hard work, self-betterment, and unpretentiousness) that they too are worthy of a royal crown. While many have commented on how lucky she is to have married Prince William, personally, I think Prince William is lucky to have married *her*.

Part of Kate's allure is that her fashion sense is pitch-perfect. She has perfected the art of "conservative chic," and her love of classic staples, like tailored suits, tweed jackets, and suede boots, makes it clear that the girl was born to be a Windsor.

In a media age full of Paris Hiltons and Orange County Housewives, Kate has shown that a girl can be both modest and sexy—and if you wear something fitted and exquisitely cut, you don't need a low neckline or short skirt. Kate has what I call the "there she is" factor—which is very different from the overly provocative "here I am" that seems to be preferred by so many modern celebrities. In fact, Kate is changing the very face of celebrity by injecting it with restraint; while others clamor to confess all, she maintains her regal silence. This is groundbreaking (if not downright radical) stuff.

I do wish Kate weren't so heavy handed with her eyeliner, but she is leading the way when it comes to teaching England the value of a good American-style blow-dry. (Seriously, Kate's blow-dry legacy is so important to the current state of British hair, the monarchy hardly needs to bother with any other charity work.)

Overall, your sartorial goal should be to attain the classic English look seen on Kate, her sister Pippa, and the other rosy-cheeked British girls that move within their affluent "Sloane Ranger" circle.

The term "Sloane Ranger" (often shortened to "Sloane") refers to young upper-class or upper-middle-class Brits who tend to congregate near Chelsea's fashionable Sloane Square (SW3). These people don't buy new things, rather they *inherit* priceless things. In the Sloane Ranger world, it's important to show that you are not a slave to fashion trends and would actually prefer to wear a vintage tweed jacket that once belonged to your grandmother than something flashy and expensive from Versace. It's also important to work a subtle predilection for the countryside into your wardrobe. Remember: It's not about looking cutting-edge; it's about looking classic. Kate has managed to do this beautifully while adding her own contemporary touches.

# Get the English Look

*Know first who you are; and then adorn yourself accordingly.*
—EPICTETUS (AD 55–AD 135)

## City Chic

London winters are not hugely cold, so no need to bust out the UGGs and Columbia ski gear. Usually a wool pea coat and leather gloves are more than warm enough, and because it rarely snows, you are free to wear heeled boots all winter long without fear of slipping on the ice. (FYI: Top Shop is great for affordable, stylish pea coats.)

Conversely, London summers aren't hugely hot, so no need for flip-flops or skimpy sunwear. Do as the Duchess of Cambridge does and spend your London days in knee-length skirts, patterned day dresses, cashmere cardigans, and wedge heels.

## Countryside Chic

Before I came to England, the words "country" and "countryside" conjured up images of tractors, hay bales, cowboy boots, and corn festivals. I was raised in a town obsessed with rodeos, livestock auctions, and Day-Glo hunting gear, and as a result I wanted to get as far away from it all as possible. I wanted sophistication, I wanted culture, I wanted *the city*.

So you can imagine my surprise when I learned that in England, the countryside *is* sophisticated! Think pitchers of Pimm's, polo matches, and cricket; think black-tie balls and hot mulled wine. There is nothing more English than walking your Labrador through a damp field on your way to the local pub, where you may or may not bump into Princess Anne.

In England, countryside means old school elegance, and thankfully there is not a ten-gallon hat or oversized belt buckle in sight. Even if you live in London, you should visit Gloucestershire or Oxfordshire at least once (while you're there, be sure to browse Prince Charles's organic farm shop at Highgrove.)

That said, countryside chic means obtaining the following essentials:

- a perfectly fitted tweed jacket (preferably from the Duchess of Cambridge's preferred designer Katherine Hooker, www .katherinehooker.com/)

- a neutral-colored cashmere sweater

- a pair of classic Wellington boots (always from Hunter and always in green)—these are vital for wet, muddy weather, www.hunter-boot.com

&bull; a quilted Barbour jacket, www.barbour.com

&bull; a newfound love for ruddy cheeks and windswept hair

## Seaside Chic

In her earlier, more casual days, Kate sported a look known as "Fulham-by-the-Sea"—meaning this is what girls who live in SW6 would wear if they were spending the afternoon enjoying a brisk walk along the Devon coast. This look is still widely popular (you guessed it) in Fulham and by the sea—both of which are worth a visit. It consists of:

&bull; designer jeans (Trilogy employs a fantastic "jean genie," which means you don't have to try on more than three pairs. www.trilogystores.co.uk)

&bull; a "puffa" (a down vest)

&bull; a pashmina (The test of a genuine wool pashmina is to thread it through a wedding ring; if it doesn't slide through easily, it's too thick, and therefore of lesser quality.)

## Nightclub Chic

If you want to get through the doors of London's elite clubs (and even better, catch the eye of one of London's elite bachelors), the royal aim here is youthful, understated elegance, *not* girls gone wild. Remember: nothing too trendy and nothing too trashy. Essential nightclub staples include:

&bull; a shift or wrap dress

&bull; two-and-a-half-inch patent or suede heels in nude or black

- a small clutch

- simple, statement jewelry

## Dressing for the Weather

*For months the sky has been a depthless gray.*
*Sometimes it rains but mostly it is just dull.*
*It's like living inside a Tupperware.*
—BILL BRYSON

I've never been the type of person to be affected by the weather. As long as I am warm enough, cool enough, or have an umbrella to protect my hair—the daily forecast has no bearing on my mood. I grew up in Colorado and I went to college in upstate New York—I've seen my fair share of blizzards and secretly enjoy them. (I never understood my college roommate who used a special UV sunlamp to stop her from plunging into depression.) So when it came to London weather, I was hardly daunted—I mean really, *how extreme could it be?*

Well, that's just it. It's not extreme at all. In fact, it's extremely tedious in its *lack* of extremes. Bright gray. Bright gray. Bright gray. Light rain. Bright gray. Bright gray. Bright gray. Light rain. Repeat ad nauseam. (In fact, I've never understood why the British are so obsessed with talking about the weather, because the weather changes so very little!)

For the first ten years, I was absolutely fine—*I was in London!* Who cares what color the sky is? But, like Chinese water torture, slowly but surely it starts to wear on you, and slowly but surely it starts to drive you quietly insane.

You don't realize how *amazing* blue skies are until you are permanently deprived of them (but on the plus side, no sunshine means no sun damage, which means you'll have great skin when you get older). On the rare occasion that the sun *does* come out, the Brits go *bonkers*: The parks are full of pale, pasty people in shorts and bikinis—all crazed with fear that if they don't sunbathe *immediately*, they may never feel the sun's warmth on their skin ever again (even if it's barely sixty degrees outside).

Which brings me to the small matter of it being approximately fifty-two to sixty-two degrees outside every single day—too cold for a sundress, too warm for chunky knits—forcing you to live in a constant state of lukewarm layers. Frustrating, but it can be done.

- Always carry an umbrella. Always.

- Always carry sunglasses. It may be gray, but it can still be bright.

- Neutral T-shirts and tank tops will become your layering staples (white, black, navy, and beige).

- Always have a coordinated second layer (cardigan, blazer, pashmina, or light raincoat).

- Learn to embrace knee-high boots and opaque tights (so you can still wear skirts when it's chilly).

- Waterproof all your shoes (especially the suede).

- Take vitamin D supplements.

- Wear blush so you don't look like a ghost (but not so much that you look like a clown).

# "Fancy Dress"

If you see this on an invitation, it does *not* mean to wear your fanciest cocktail dress; it means that you are required to dress in costume, and the costume in question is usually bizarrely themed (e.g., "Dress as Your Favorite Tube Station," "Dress as Your Favorite Vegetable," etc—the wackier the better and the more the Brits seem to love it). When I first moved to England, I didn't quite understand the constant British obsession with costume parties. Prior to landing on UK shores, the last time I remembered going to a party where a costume was required (other than Halloween) I was in third grade. But in London I suddenly found myself attending fancy dress parties practically every month. I once went to a party themed "Dress as Your Hero," and because I went as Grace Kelly, thankfully I still managed to wear my fanciest cocktail dress.

# UK Sizes

For some reason there are only four sizes in this country: 8, 10, 12, and 14. (Apparently larger sizes exist, but I have never seen them out on the racks. Ever. )

I'm petite, but I'm pear-shaped, so I have to buy small tops and larger bottoms. In America, I wear a size 4 blouse and size 6 pants. In the UK, I wear a size 8 blouse and trousers in size 12. So as a general rule, double the size of what you wore in America and that will usually give you your size in the UK.

Shoes can be even trickier because there are UK and European sizes and they are both totally different from US sizes.

| US CLOTHING SIZE | UK CLOTHING SIZE |
|:---:|:---:|
| 0 | 4 |
| 2 | 6 |
| 4 | 8 |
| 6 | 10 |
| 8 | 12 |
| 10 | 14 |
| 12 | 16 |

| US SHOE SIZE | UK SHOE SIZE | EUROPEAN SHOE SIZE |
|:---:|:---:|:---:|
| 5.5 | 3 | 36 |
| 6.6 | 4 | 37 |
| 7.5 | 5 | 38 |
| 8.5 | 6 | 39 |
| 9.5 | 7 | 40 |
| 10.5 | 8 | 41 |

# Savvy Shopping

If I were you, I'd buy most of my clothes in America. I know it sounds weird, but I'm serious. Certain American stores are good at producing relatively inexpensive pieces of good quality that are simple and classic, with a fashionably preppy twist. Even if the only stores you hit are Banana Republic, Ann Taylor, and J.Crew, the clothes will be at least 30 percent cheaper than in the UK, and you won't look like every other girl in London, who's draped in a hodgepodge of catwalk knockoffs that will go out of style within the month. To their credit, British girls are unabashedly *experimental* when it comes to their fashion choices, and no one could accuse them of not being *individualistic*. Some even look quite *cool*. But classy?

This is where you come in. American women are world renowned for their classic grooming, their understated elegance, and their overall polish. Which is precisely why all those lonely Jude Law types will be so intrigued to meet you . . .

If you can't resist shopping in the UK (and believe me, very few can resist), don't walk straight into Burberry and Aquascutum. I love these stores (How can you not? Have you seen the guys in their ad campaigns?), but there are more enduring ways to spend your precious pence.

The UK is unique in that it has a fabulous "high street" line of shops. "High street" is another way of saying "main street"—and shops found on the high street (as opposed to Bond Street!*) are much more affordable than their couture counterparts.

My favorite of the high street chains is L.K. Bennett. Any piece from this ladylike yet quintessentially British store (be it a coat, a dress, a handbag, or a pair of peep-toe heels) will last you forever and is guaranteed to be acceptable for any English social occasion. (You'll note that the Duchess of Cambridge agrees with me, as many of her most worn accessories come from here.) www .lkbennett.com†

ALSO TRY:

- Hobbs (for fitted suits and gorgeous day dresses), www .hobbs.co.uk/

---

* Bond Street is the London equivalent of Rodeo Drive.

† Breaking news: L.K. Bennett stores are new open in Atlanta, Chicago, Houston, Philadelphia, and New York.

- Brora (for exquisite Scottish cashmere; these sweaters last *decades* without a trace of pilling), www.brora.co.uk

- Joules (for fun, country casuals), www.joules.com

- Russell & Bromley (for classic city boots) www.russellandbromley.co.uk

- Blue Velvet (for beautiful, affordable ballet flats) www.bluevelvetshoes.com

BEST AREAS FOR SHOPPING:

- Covent Garden

- High Street Kensington

- King's Road

- Marylebone High Street (Be sure to stop at Daunts book-shop while you're there—pure bookworm bliss.)

- Regent's Street

- Richmond (George Street and Hill Rise)

SHOPPING AREAS TO AVOID:

- Harrods (too touristy!—although you should at least see the Food Hall once in your lifetime)

- Knightsbridge (too touristy!)

- New Bond Street (too expensive—but fun to window shop)

- Oxford Street (too crowded! and too touristy!)

- Portobello Road (unless you like flea markets)

- Sloane Street (too expensive—but fun to window shop)

- Westfield Shopping Centre (London is a city where you shop on the street, never at the mall.)

## American Beauty

*There are no ugly women,*
*only lazy women.*
—HELENA RUBINSTEIN

This summer I was sitting in the beer garden of a pleasant West London pub, when I spotted two women sharing a bottle of white wine.

The girl on the left was wearing well-fitting jeans and a simple navy-and-white striped T-shirt; her hair was clean and sprinkled with a few impeccably placed highlights; her nails were neatly trimmed and painted nude pink. She had a larger than average nose, but her cheeks had color and her skin tone was even. Her makeup was expertly applied, and her large eyes and perfect lips were subtly emphasized so that her natural beauty shone through.

The girl on the right was wearing a patterned dress in a style that was considered "in this season" but that absolutely did not suit her figure. (I could tell that she definitely cared about and put an effort into what she was wearing; she just had no clue what colors and proportions were appropriate for her body.) Her dark hair was slightly greasy and sloppily tied back. She was blessed with pretty features, but her complexion was pasty and her eyeliner was badly smudged, which gave her a subtle panda-like look.

I couldn't hear their voices, but I had a hunch that one was American and one was British, so I walked past their table to see if I was correct—and of course I was.

Can *you* guess which girl was which?

While the Brits love fashion, they haven't quite caught up with Americans when it comes to hair, makeup, and overall grooming. I'm not quite sure why this is. It might be because salon services are twice as expensive as they are in America. (For instance, a pedicure of mediocre quality costs roughly $100.) It might be because British women simply don't know *how* to blow-dry their hair or the correct way to apply concealer. Or it might be that a long, long time ago, the only women in England that bothered do their hair and makeup were prostitutes—and so for many years afterward, any woman who dared to paint her nails was deemed an automatic whore. Thankfully, attitudes like this have moved on somewhat, but whatever the reason, the natural American urge to look pristinely polished has not yet been wholly embraced by British women.

To their credit, there are some British women who have been blessed with shiny, maintenance-free hair (that requires neither products nor heat-styling to look gorgeous) and startlingly clear skin that glows without the help of blush or pressed powder. A girl like this is what you might call a true English rose. Excellent examples are Sophie Dahl, Rosamund Pike, Kate Winslet, and of course our beloved Duchess of Cambridge. (In fact, the lovely Kate is so unusually well polished she's practically an honorary American.)

However, on the streets of London, girls like these are few and far between; everyone else you encounter looks like Kate Moss or Amy Winehouse the morning after. Meaning, everyone else needs

The Duchess of Windsor (formerly Wallis Simpson)
with her husband, Prince Edward,
the Duke of Windsor, on their wedding day.

Wallis Simpson, an American socialite, was hardly known for her beauty, yet she was always immaculately groomed. What happened to her? She married the heir to the British throne.

The lesson? American grooming makes you luminous. Use it to your advantage. (And just so you know, if Prince Harry falls for an American girl, there is absolutely nothing in the law that says he has to abdicate.)

For more on Wallis Simpson and her royal love affair see "Royal FAQ's," p. 108 and "Your Crush is Nothing New," p. 118

to wash their hair, clean their nails, shave their legs, and not be so heavy-handed with their eye makeup. And for the love of god, please don't wear chipped toenail polish in public.

This is where you will shine as an American. Without even trying, your daily beauty habits will *already* be eons ahead of most of your London counterparts. And for this reason, you *will* get noticed by Londoners of the opposite sex. When faced with your perfect yet subtle manicure, faultless blow-dry, and flawlessly applied natural makeup, they just can't help themselves.

> *American girls are livelier, better educated . . . not*
> *as squeamish as their English sisters . . . and*
> *better able to take care of themselves.*
> —THE PRINCE OF WALES, 1930

## BEAUTY BASICS

- When it comes to makeup, always strive for a classic, *understated* look. The real key to makeup is that it shouldn't look like you're wearing makeup—it just looks like *you* (only slightly better).

- Understand the shape of your face. The way you apply eye shadow and blush may not work for me because our cheekbones and brow bones are shaped differently. So just because you like your friend's makeup doesn't mean it's the right makeup technique for you.

- See a professional. I went to a MAC makeup counter when I was sixteen years old, and although I don't use all of their products (I'm still a fan of Maybelline!), nearly twenty years later I still use many of the same application techniques that

I learned that day. So choose a cosmetic counter and book an appointment. Tell the makeup artist that you want a natural, understated *daytime* look. If you're not happy with the result, go somewhere else until you are.

- Take care of your skin. Even if you stay out till three in the morning clubbing the night away with Prince Harry—make sure you cleanse, tone, and moisturize before falling into bed.

- Embrace the power of concealer. There is no point slaving away with foundation, blush, and eye makeup if those tiny imperfections are still on display. So cover up those dark circles and tiny red spots before you do anything else. I also use concealer to cover up the annoying redness in the creases of my nose and across the entire surface of my eyelids.

- Always apply makeup in natural light. (Because badly applied makeup is a great deal worse than no makeup.)

- Take care of your eyes. I use eye cream at bedtime and eye gel first thing in the morning. Always use your ring finger (because it's the weakest) when applying anything under your eyes and always use outward motions to avoid causing wrinkles.

- Even your skin tone. Unless you have super dry skin, use a powder-based (not liquid) foundation to avoid greasiness. I love MAC's Studio Fix.

- Achieve English rosiness with the perfect powder blush—make sure it matches your skin tone perfectly or it can look dirty. Apply blush to the apple of your cheek—where the sun would naturally hit.

- Long to look like Diana? Don't attempt to create doleful princess eyes by wearing lots of 1980s blue eyeliner. And while we all love Kate Middleton, many experts agree that her thick eyeliner is a bit heavy-handed. For a look that is soft yet defined, try lining your eyes with dark brown shadow instead of heavy liquid and apply it with a small angled brush (MAC #263). Also try shadow to color your brows instead of greasy pencils.

- Forget what all the magazines say about "this season's" eye shadow colors—the only colors that belong on your face should be muted and natural (think gray, brown, beige, apricot, cream). Unless we're talking about your actual, God-given irises, stay away from blue, green, and purple.

- Expensive doesn't always mean better. I use mascara from Max Factor and instead of lip gloss, I use Vaseline! Once you've found something that works for you, stay loyal. There is no point in spending money on dozens of dazzling new products that you'll probably never use more than once. (Besides, your bathroom cabinet in London won't be big enough to hold them.)

- Beware of shine! Especially in a damp, humid city like London. Carry blotting papers or find a good translucent powder that doesn't build up with each application. I'm a lifelong devotee to Maybelline's Shine Free Oil Control Pressed Powder (a bargain at $7.99!).

- Top Travel Tip: Always pack your makeup in your carry-on bag. If your luggage gets lost, and you're forced to borrow your friend's clothes for forty-eight hours (or worse, keep wearing the clothes that you flew in), at least you know that your face will still look normal. There is nothing more awful than borrowing cosmetics that don't match your skin tone or frantically scouring drugstores in another country for beauty brands that they probably don't sell. (Alas, Sephora has not yet made it to England.)

* As we all know, *true* beauty comes from the soul—and will shine through with or without perfectly applied makeup; it comes from your smile, your laugh, and your kindness toward others.

# Getting Your Head Around Hats and Fascinators

*Where did you get that hat?*
—PRINCE PHILIP TO QUEEN ELIZABETH II
AFTER HER CORONATION, 1953

I'll never forget my very first hat purchase. I was twenty-three years old and it was for, not surprisingly, my very first visit to Royal Ascot. I just kept thinking of the Ascot lyrics from *My Fair Lady* that went, "Every duke and earl and peer is here. Everyone who should be here is here . . . " and I was more determined than ever to get the look right. In the beginning, I headed straight to Self-ridges (Princess Diana's favorite department store), which is famous for its hat department. It was pure heaven. Your posture improves, your cheekbones are framed . . . I mean, it really is amazing what

a flying saucer–shaped brim or a bit of netting draped over your eyes can do for a girl. However, my hair is naturally quite big, so I needed to opt for something simple. (Only girls with straight hair can pull off elaborate millinery.)

Still, I nearly hyperventilated when I discovered that every hat I liked cost nearly $1,000. So the next day, after work, I headed to (you guessed it) John Lewis. Their hat department proved to be just as large as Selfridges's, except everything was under $100. I chose a classic straw hat in a neutral peach, with a large beige twist at the front (which I knew would perfectly match my champagne silk Ann Taylor suit) and headed home, proud to be holding my very first hatbox.

The problem was that two of my British girlfriends called me right as I was leaving the store and told me to meet them for drinks at a Mayfair bar only three streets away. I was hardly going to let a giant hexagonal hatbox keep me from my cocktails, so off I went, and one drink led to another that led to another, and before I knew what was happening we let a group of cute English boys take us to a nightclub.

If you've never drunkenly pleaded with a coat check attendant at 3 a.m. on a Tuesday night to please let you have your hat even though you lost your ticket, because it's Ascot Ladies Day tomorrow—then you clearly haven't lived.

(Not in London anyway.)

HATS . . .

- Are for English races and English weddings. Nothing else.

- Should be classy and fabulous, but should not hide or overpower your face. (A good rule of thumb is that the brim should not extend beyond your shoulder line.)

- Should be worn at home first; experiment with various angles until you get it right. (Historically, a lady wore her hat tipped to the right side of her head so that her face was visible to gentleman friends clutching her left arm as they escorted her.)

- Should be worn with confidence and nonchalance; if you feel awkward or uncomfortable, choose something smaller and more subtle, like a fascinator.

- Should complement your dress and vice versa; if you're wearing a bold dress, opt for a more discreet headpiece. Likewise, a dazzling fascinator works better with a simple dress.

- Should be fastened securely on your head. You want to spend the day sipping champagne, not clutching your headpiece. When in doubt, buy some bobby pins (or "hairgrips" as they're called in the UK).

- Should not be too theatrical. Not everyone can be Lady Gaga. And that's a good thing. (I think it's fair to say that Princess Beatrice learned that lesson for us all.)

- Can be expensive. If you can't afford to buy one, rent one! There are several hat hire shops in London. My favorite is Hectic Hat Hire in Fulham, www.hectichathire.co.uk.

It's my wedding day. I'm standing near the doors of the tiny London chapel in my giant white satin gown, awaiting the musical cue for my dad to escort me down the aisle. I can't see them yet, but I know the chapel is filled with one hundred of our closest friends and family—half of them American, half of them British. The aisle is lined with bay trees (a decorative touch later borrowed by William and Kate). My five bridesmaids, dressed in gold damask, slowly begin the procession ahead of me. The last one in line turns to me, and right before she walks down the aisle, she says, "Jerramy, just so you know—there are lots of girls in there with birds on their heads!"

What my dearest American bridesmaid didn't know is that those birds were actually fetching British headpieces known as *fascinators*. Fascinators are feathery little head ornaments, held in place with a comb, pin, or band, that are becoming more and more popular with young British women who want to avoid feeling like Lady Bracknell* in large, wide-brimmed headwear. Because I'm so short and tend to look like a mushroom in wide-brimmed hats, I am also a huge fan of the fascinator. As is, increasingly so, the Duchess of Cambridge. Despite their frivolous appearance, this relatively recent millinery trend shows no signs of abating.

FASCINATORS . . .

- Should be worn on the side of your head; never in the center. When netting is involved, it's okay to let it drape seductively over one eye.

---

* If you don't know who Lady Bracknell is, you need to read *The Importance of Being Earnest* by Oscar Wilde. Now.

🐜 Work well with wavy hair, tumbling curls, or an elegant up-do. Experiment to see which angle will best complement your features and your outfit.

🐜 Should remain on your head throughout the day and night, regardless of where you are—be it a church, formal dining room, or dance floor.

🐜 Can easily veer from classy and decorative to flamboyant and inappropriate, so ask a friend to make sure you look like you're going to a wedding and not a Brazilian Carnival.

## Wedding Guest Chic

*Charles (played by Hugh Grant):*
How do you do—my name is Charles.
*Old man:* Don't be ridiculous, Charles died twenty years ago!
*Charles:* Must be a different Charles, I think.
*Old man:* Are you telling me I don't know my own brother?
—FROM THE FILM *FOUR WEDDINGS AND A FUNERAL* (1994)

*Four Weddings and a Funeral* is not just a terrific Hugh Grant movie—when it comes to understanding the wacky and wonderful occasion that is a British wedding, it's practically a documentary. While US weddings are incredibly diverse, British weddings tend to follow a very predictable format:

🐜 There is no rehearsal dinner whatsoever, but the bachelor/bachelorette parties ("stag" and "hen" weekends, respectively) usually require at least two nights away in a foreign country.

❧ The ceremony takes place in the bride's village church and involves several tuneless hymns that only the privately educated Brits know the words to.*

❧ The reception is held in a marquee in the backyard of the bride's parents.

❧ You have champagne and canapés for one hour and then you begin a three-course sit-down dinner which is weirdly called the "wedding breakfast."

❧ You are rarely seated next to your date or your spouse, yet you are always seated boy-girl-boy-girl.

❧ You talk to the guy on your right (and no one else) for the entire first course; when the main course arrives, you can begin talking to the person on your left (and no one else). When the dessert arrives, you can talk to anyone at the table.

❧ After all three courses have been served and consumed, the speeches begin. Speeches are considered way, way more important in Britain than they are in America—people make serious bets over both their content and their length.

❧ There are always three speeches and they are always in the same order: the father of the bride, the best man, and then the groom (as if he doesn't have enough going on that day). The British guests at my wedding nearly hyperventilated

---

* I suggest learning the words and tune to "Jerusalem" and "I Vow to Thee My Country"—as you'll be hearing them for the rest of your life.

when two of my bridesmaids got up to speak.* (Women giving speeches? That's crazy!)

- It is not uncommon for each speech to last well over thirty minutes. Please take note that you are still sitting at a table full of strangers, you've been sitting at this table for nearly three hours already, and you have absolutely nothing to do but continue sitting there until the speeches are over and the wedding cake is served, so most people think that to pass the time they might as well get drunk.

- Yes, cake is served *after, and in addition to,* dessert—and it's *always* brandy-soaked fruit cake with a two-inch layer of marzipan icing.

- English wedding cake is soaked in so much alcohol that it has what appears to be an infinite shelf life. It's very common for British couples to serve actual pieces of their wedding cake at their first child's christening. That's how long this scary cake can last.

- Finally, around 1 a.m., the dancing begins, by which point everyone is either (a) asleep on the table or (b) too drunk to stand up.

All British weddings follow this exact same formula. Because any "personalized" touches are considered to be distastefully inappropriate and/or a nouveau break with tradition, all UK weddings

---

* Actually, having adult bridesmaids at all is a purely American phenomenon. Traditionally, British brides (including Princess Diana) have tiny flower girls only. But I'm fairly sure Pippa Middleton broke that trend once and for all.

become virtually indistinguishable. So when the gorgeous Hugh Grant shows up late to the church, slides into the pew at the last minute, and mumbles, "Who is it today?"—you really can't blame him.

## Replying to Wedding Invitations

British wedding invitations do not come with RSVP cards. Your response must be handwritten on nice (preferably headed) stationery in the *third person*, using the standard, traditional wording of a formal reply.

For example:

> *Miss Annabel Swan [that's you] would like to thank Mr. and Mrs. Blueblood for the kind invitation to the marriage of their daughter, Penelope, to Mr. Hugh Grant at St. Paul's Cathedral on Saturday 29th July, 2012, at 3 o'clock, and afterwards at Claridge's Hotel, and is delighted to accept/regrets that she is unable to attend.*

You do not sign your name, there is no salutation, and the date is written at the bottom left of the page. The envelope is traditionally addressed to the bride's mother or to the host(s) whose name is on the invitation.

## The Dress Code

Describing the dress code for a British wedding is difficult. They are not black-tie optional affairs, so the slinky evening cocktail dresses that you wear to weddings in America usually don't work.

(In fact, the Brits think it's ridiculous that Americans wear tuxedos and evening dresses to church weddings.) Instead, think of a British wedding as going to a very formal church garden party—which is essentially what it is . . .

- Traditionally, wedding attire for men is "morning dress." For the longest time I thought this was "mourning dress" and found the idea rather depressing, until I found out that "morning" actually refers to the time of day that the suit is to be worn. Basically, a morning suit is the daytime equivalent of a tuxedo and is worn to formal events that take place in the day, like weddings, royal garden parties, and the Royal Enclosure at Ascot. A morning suit consists of a tailcoat, vest, tie, and striped trousers. Most British men own their own morning suit (most also own their own tuxedo). If your date doesn't have one, encourage him to rent one; otherwise a dark suit with a shirt and tie will suffice.

- Women should wear an elegant suit or chic, yet conservative day dress with neutral shoes. Getting too matchy matchy can look tacky.

- Head-to-toe outfits in white or cream should never be worn, and all black, unless cleverly accessorized, is often too somber and usually discouraged.

- Hats and fascinators are traditional, but not compulsory.

- Usually the outfit you wear to Ascot or Henley would also be appropriate for a British wedding.

- When in doubt, wear anything from Hobbs or L.K. Bennett.

- If someone is wearing a dress identical to yours, don't ignore the situation. Approach her with a smile and compliment her on her good taste.

RECOMMENDED READING:

### *A Guide to Elegance* by Genevieve Antoine Dariaux

Originally published in 1964 (the pinnacle of *Mad Men*–like style), this book is a bona fide bible for anyone hoping to attain timeless chic, grace, and ballerina-grade poise. From "Accessories" to "Zippers," Madame Dariaux imparts her pearls of wisdom on all things fashion-related.

### *Elegance* by Kathleen Tessaro

I love this novel. It's the story of an American girl living in London (can you tell why I love this novel?) whose miserable expat existence is transformed when she discovers a dusty, antique book entitled, *A Guide to Elegance* by Genevieve Dariaux. What unfolds is a hilarious, contemporary version of Pygmalion—and the protagonist is a girl after my own heart, because she very much becomes her own Professor Higgins.

# FOUR

# ROYAL ENCOUNTERS

L ots of people I know don't like talking about the millennium mainly because they feel their New Year's Eve party that night was kind of a letdown.

Not me.

Through serendipity and a huge, rather magical stroke of luck, I spent New Year's Eve 1999 in a royal palace. A real one, with a real living, breathing royal family. Turns out that one of my friends from college was actually the nephew of a maharaja, and as a result I had been invited to spend the millennium with his family at their palace in India. Needless to say, it was one of the single most amazing experiences of my life.

I stayed in the palace for two weeks, and one night at dinner I was seated next to the Maharaja. I'd been to a cocktail party beforehand, and after four straight hours of gin and tonics, I remember wondering how on earth I was going to make sparkling conversation with a royal patriarch through an eight-course formal dinner—all while making sure I was sipping my soup in the right direction! Thank god that I had been studying etiquette* for years (and thank god for those gin and tonics!).

Still, the Maharaja had held his title since he was four years old and certainly he'd had wackier dinner companions than me in his time, so I tried not to worry. (As expected, His Highness was extremely friendly, and his superb social skills made it incredibly easy for me.)

But my point is that you never know where life will take you. You might think sitting next to royalty at dinner will never happen to you in a million years.

But it can. And it might. So make sure you're ready . . .

## Meeting the Queen

Don't discount this. You never know when Her Majesty might appear before you! The Royal Family is much more relaxed these days than they were even ten years ago, so there's no reason to panic. Still, whether your royal encounter is impromptu or planned, it's best to be prepared.

- When Her Majesty enters the room, all stand.

- I shouldn't have to say this, but make sure you are not chewing gum.

- One never introduces oneself to the Queen; one must always wait to be formally presented.

---

* Originally, the French word "etiquette" referred to the set of instructions that dictated how to behave properly at Court, which was rather apt in these circumstances!

- Curtsey. Americans are not subjects of the Queen and therefore *technically* not required to curtsey like Canadians, Australians, and other members of the Commonwealth, but it remains a traditional and valued sign of respect.

- Verbally address the Queen as "Your Majesty" in the first instance, then "ma'am"—to rhyme with spam.

- In conversation, substitute "Your Majesty" for the word "you."

- Do not offer your hand or touch the monarch in any way. However, if the Queen offers her hand, take it briefly and lightly—no bone crunching handshakes.

- If the Queen chooses to engage in polite conversation with you, allow her to lead the conversation. As much as you're dying to ask about that naughty, redheaded grandson of hers—questions of any kind are not permitted.

- Curtsey again as she leaves you.

In the years that followed, I found myself face-to-face with the Princess Royal, Earl Spencer, and the Duchess of York, among others. (Like I said, don't think it won't happen to you, because it will!). Keeping the correct forms of address in mind, the above protocol applies to meeting all high-ranking members of the Royal Family, but strictness varies according to the formality of setting (i.e. meeting Prince Harry at a charity reception is very different from meeting him at a nightclub). If there is any doubt over the formality preferred by a member of the Royal Family, contact the appropriate private secretary.

> *Curtsey while you're thinking. It saves time.*
> —THE QUEEN OF HEARTS, *ALICE IN WONDERLAND*

#### HOW TO CURTSEY

- A court curtsey is always made with your weight on your right foot and the toe of your left foot a few inches behind your right heel.

- As you bend your right knee, your body gently sinks.

- Your arms should be gracefully bent, and your hands should be occupied in lightly holding your skirt or gown.

- Lower your eyes briefly but resume eye contact when you rise.

- A curtsey should be done gracefully and with control. If executed correctly, a curtsey feels a bit like like a ballet move.

- Practice curtseying from a standing position and (because sometimes your royal moment will need to happen quickly) also practice walking into it, leading with your right foot.

## Royal Invitations

A royal invitation is a *command*—a command that you have the honor to obey. (The Queen's commands can only be refused in the case of illness.)

In the past, if one were to attend the Court of St. James's,* men

---

* The royal Court of St. James's is considered to sit wherever the British monarch happens to be.

would wear knee breeches while women were obliged to wear tiaras and dresses with trains. Luckily, the rules governing formal court dress have relaxed a bit, and Buckingham Palace will tell you that there is no official dress code. But there are two regal events that still require some sartorial knowledge:

## The Queen's Garden Party

Held every summer on the grounds of Buckingham Palace, these elite social events are infamous. Just imagine a glorious afternoon filled with military bands, massive tea tents, and hundreds of specially chosen guests milling around the enormous palace lawn hoping to be spoken to by Her Majesty. I've waited years for someone I know to invite me along as a guest!

When I found out that my best gay friend had been invited, I nearly kissed him! At long last, I was going to be introduced to the Queen! *Finally!* Then my friend confessed that he was taking his mum to the party instead of me. I nearly killed him.

Nevertheless, I plan to attend a Queen's Garden Party in my lifetime—and so should you. Here is the dress code for when that day arrives: Men invited to Buckingham Palace should wear their military uniform or morning coat. Women should wear a smart day dress with a hat or fascinator. Unlike Henley, there is not an official hemline restriction, though you should always plan to err on the side of good taste and avoid anything above the knee.

## State Banquets

Most state banquets are "white tie," which is even more formal than black tie. Men wear evening tailcoats, white bow ties, white waistcoats, and starched wing collar shirts. Women wear floor-length evening gowns and gloves (it is best not to wear black, which is really only appropriate when the Court is in mourning). If you own a tiara, this is the time to wear it. When dining with the Queen, please note that she sits first, eats first, and when she finishes eating, you should stop too.

## The Loyal Toast

The Loyal Toast is a traditional toast given before a formal, state, or military dinner. The toast is usually initiated and recited by the principal host before being repeated by the assembled guests in unison—all of whom are standing. It consists simply of the words *"The Queen!"* You raise your glass for the toast, take a sip, and then sit down.

Occasionally, there is a second loyal toast immediately following the first: "To the Prince Philip, Duke of Edinburgh, the Prince of Wales, and the other members of the Royal Family."

## Titles

A member of royalty is a king, queen, prince, or princess. All other aristocrats are members of what is known as the British *Peerage*. The Peerage has five hereditary degrees, each one outranking the next: duke, marquess,* earl, viscount,† and baron. Baronets and

---

* Pronounced *mar-kwiss.*

† The *s* is not pronounced in viscount. It should rhyme with *my count*, not *discount.*

knights are not peers. A royal or a peer can also hold more than one separate peerage. (For example, His Royal Highness Prince William is also the Duke of Cambridge, the Earl of Strathearn, the Baron Carrickfergus, and a Royal Knight Companion of the Most Noble Order of the Garter.)

If someone is "The Honourable," it means he or she is the younger son of an earl, or the child or daughter-in-law of a viscount or baron. Do not use the title in speech, only in writing, when it is abbreviated to "The Hon."

## Forms of Address

Titles and the correct address for conversational use:

| | |
|---|---|
| KING/ QUEEN | Your Majesty, then sir or ma'am |
| PRINCE / PRINCESSES OR ANYONE THAT HAS HRH BEFORE HIS OR HER NAME | Your Royal Highness, then sir or ma'am |
| DUKE /DUCHESS | Your Grace, then Duke/ Duchess |
| MARQUESS / MARCHIONESS* | Your Grace, then Lord/ Lady So-and-so |
| EARL/ COUNTESS | My Lord/Madam, then Lord/ Lady So-and-so |
| VISCOUNT/ VISCOUNTESS | My Lord/Madam, then Lord/ Lady So-and-so |

* Pronounced *marshoness.*

| BARON/ BARONESS | My Lord/Madam, then Lord/ Lady So-and-so |
|---|---|
| BARONET/ BARONETESS | Sir or Dame |
| KNIGHT/ DAME | Sir or Dame |

NOTE: If you are invited to a stately home, never use the words "House," "Hall," etc, when referring to it. "I'm going to Downton" implies that you are the guest of Lord Grantham. "I'm going to Downton Abbey" indicates that you will be paying an entrance fee.

## The British Line of Succession

The British throne cannot be inherited by anyone who is not blood-related to the sovereign—this includes Camilla, Duchess of Cornwall and Catherine, Duchess of Cambridge—who are part of the Royal Family through marriage only and therefore not listed in the line of succession.

In 2011, the British government, along with the sixteen Commonwealth countries, voted to overturn a thousand years of royal history by finally allowing the eldest child (male *or* female) to inherit the throne. Up until then the British monarchy had yet to change their rather sexist rule of primogeniture*—where succes-

---

* Many agree that primogeniture was sexist, discriminatory, and outdated; nonetheless, it has produced some of the most successful and longest reigning female monarchs in history, including Queen Elizabeth I, Queen Victoria, and Queen Elizabeth II herself.

# The Windsor Family Tree

(No need to memorize the whole thing, but you should at least be able to name the Queen's four children)

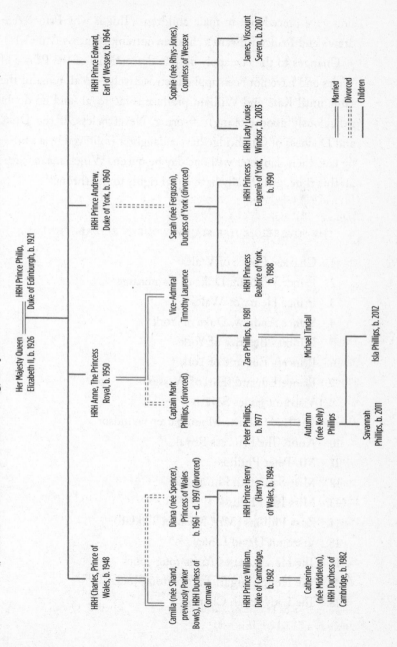

sion gave precedence to male children. (This is why Prince Andrew's and Prince Edward's children outrank Princess Anne's.)

Changes to the law apply only to descendents of the Prince of Wales and have not been applied retroactively—so all remains the same until Kate and William produce some royal (and no doubt ridiculously good-looking) offspring. Nevertheless, if the Duke and Duchess of Cambridge have a daughter (followed by a son)—by law, their daughter will one day be queen. Which means after all this time, girls finally have equal rights to the throne!

### THE SOVEREIGN: HER MAJESTY QUEEN ELIZABETH II

1. Charles, Prince of Wales
2. Prince William, Duke of Cambridge
3. Prince Henry of Wales
4. Prince Andrew, Duke of York
5. Princess Beatrice of York
6. Princess Eugenie of York
7. Prince Edward, Earl of Wessex
8. Viscount James Severn
9. The Lady Louise Mountbatten-Windsor
10. Anne, The Princess Royal
11. Mr. Peter Phillips
12. Miss Savannah Phillips
13. Miss Isla Phillips
14. Zara Phillips (Mrs. Michael Tindall)
15. Viscount David Linley
16. The Hon. Charles Armstrong-Jones
17. The Hon. Margarita Armstrong-Jones
18. The Lady Sarah Chatto

19. Master Samuel Chatto
20. Master Arthur Chatto
21. The Duke of Gloucester
22. Earl of Ulster
23. Lord Culloden
24. The Lady Cosima Windsor
25. The Lady Davina Lewis
26. Miss Senna Lewis
27. The Lady Rose Gilman
28. Miss Lyla Gilman
29. The Duke of Kent
30. The Lady Amelia Windsor
31. The Lady Helen Taylor
32. Master Columbus Taylor
33. Master Cassius Taylor
34. Miss Eloise Taylor
35. Miss Estella Taylor
36. The Hon. Albert Windsor
37. The Hon. Leopold Windsor
38. The Lord Frederick Windsor
39. The Lady Gabriella Windsor
40. Princess Alexandra, the Hon Lady Ogilvy

# Royal FAQs

Why isn't Philip the King if he's married to the Queen? Why isn't Kate a princess if she's married to a prince? Is he the Prince of Cambridge or the Duke of Wales? How can she be Princess Michael of Kent? That's a man's name! And so on. No matter how hard we try, Americans can't help but struggle to understand the intricacies of the British aristocracy. And who can blame us? When you're born in a land where no one is a sir or lord, much less a prince or princess, the very idea of titles that elevate one person over another can be difficult to grasp. That said, I've done my best to shine some light on the most popular royal questions Americans tend to ask me . . .

**Q: Now that Kate is married to Prince William, why isn't she called Princess Catherine?**

A: Princess titles are tricky. If they are not inherited (as is the case with Princess Beatrice and Princess Eugenie), the woman's first name cannot be part of the actual title. Diana was *not* Princess Diana—that's just what we liked to call her. She was The Princess of Wales. Camilla is *not* Duchess Camilla—she is The Duchess of Cornwall. Royal brides do not inherit titles; they merely assume the full title of their royal husband. (However, men do not assume the titles of women—which is why the Queen's husband, Prince Philip, is not king). When Catherine Middleton married Prince William, she technically became Princess William of Wales (yes, a man's name!) and would have retained this title if William had not received a dukedom as a wedding gift from the Queen. Since William became the Duke of Cambridge, protocol required that Catherine become the Duchess of Cambridge. (Prince William is also Earl of Strathearn and Baron Carrickfergus, meaning Kate is also Countess of Strathearn and Baroness Carrickfergus.) But Kate is *not* Princess Catherine and she is *not* Duchess Catherine; rather she is officially known as HRH The Duchess of Cambridge.

**Q: If Diana had lived, would she have become queen? What about Camilla and Catherine — will they one day become queen?**

A: Technically, yes. If Diana had remained married to Prince Charles when he became king, she would have become his queen consort and known as Queen Diana. However, Charles and Diana divorced in 1996, making this outcome impossible.

Camilla, currently The Duchess of Cornwall, will technically be entitled to become queen consort and Queen Camilla, but out of respect for Diana's memory it is suspected that she will choose to remain a duchess. When Prince William becomes king, The Duchess of Cambridge will become queen consort and probably be known as Queen Catherine.

**Q: Can the Queen choose to skip Prince Charles and pass the throne directly to Prince William?**

A: No. The Queen does not have a historic or constitutional right to do such a thing. As it stands, her eldest son, Prince Charles, is next in line to the throne and will become King of England when the Queen dies. Any alteration to the line of succession would require a constitutional change to be voted through the UK parliament and throughout the Commonwealth.

**Q: What is William and Harry's last name? Is it Wales or Windsor?**

A: Neither. Members of the Royal Family who are titled His (or Her) Royal Highness do not use a last name. Their official *titles* are HRH Prince William of Wales and HRH Prince Henry (Harry) of Wales, but titles are not last names—and "Windsor" is simply the royal house to which the brothers belong. However, throughout their time with the Armed Forces, both princes wanted to simplify things and decided to use the last name "Wales" during all training and active duty.

**Q: Why are some royals given titles like Princess of Wales or Duchess of Cambridge when they are neither from Wales nor from Cambridge?**

A: The Queen bestowed all four of her children with special titles—Charles is Prince of Wales, Andrew is Duke of York, Edward is Earl of Wessex, Anne is Princess Royal. Women who marry royal men automatically take on the title: Diana became Princess of Wales, Fergie became Duchess of York, Sophie became Countess of Wessex—but Captain Mark Phillips, who married Princess Anne, got nothing because titles don't pass through females.

In the same way, when William became the Duke of Cambridge, Kate became the Duchess of Cambridge. When Camilla married Charles, Prince of Wales, the palace worried there would be public outcry if Camilla became the new Princess of Wales, supplanting Diana's legacy. So even though Camilla is technically permitted to take on this title, she insists that we call her the Duchess of Cornwall, because Charles is also the Duke of Cornwall.

All of these places—Wales, York, Wessex, Cambridge, Cornwall—are found in Great Britain, and since the monarchy reigns over all of Great Britain and Northern Ireland, it doesn't really matter if they have specific residences in these areas.

**Q: What is the difference between the Queen and the Queen Mother?**

A: The British throne cannot be inherited by anyone who is not blood-related to the sovereign, hence the title Queen Mother (or "Queen Mum") is reserved for the widowed (or *dowager*) queen consort whose son or daughter is the reigning monarch. For example, when Princess Elizabeth's father (George VI) died, she inherited the throne and became Queen Elizabeth II—while her widowed mother (portrayed by Helena Bonham Carter in *The King's Speech)*, who married into the Royal Family, became "the Queen Mum." If Diana had remained married to Charles and he'd left her widowed, she would also have been the Queen Mum. Currently, if Prince Charles becomes king and dies before Camilla, Prince William will become king, but it is not yet clear if Camilla will become Queen Mother since Prince William is not actually her son. If Prince Willliam becomes king and dies before his wife, Kate will become the Queen Mother and their eldest child will become the reigning monarch.

**Q: How come Princess Anne's children don't have titles?**

A: Although rules to the royal succession recently changed, every other title requires a separate Act of Parliament to change in a similar way. And as things currently stand, royal titles only pass through the male line. Because of this, Princess Anne's son, Peter, and daughter, Zara, do not have titles. Princess Anne declined to have further titles bestowed on her children by the Queen, hoping this would help them to lead normal lives. Moreover, Peter did not inherit a courtesy title from his father, because Captain Phillips also declined a title from the Queen upon his marriage to Princess Anne.

Hence, Princess Anne's children remain Mr. Phillips and Mrs. Michael Tindall. (Though I'm not entirely convinced this has allowed them to lead "normal" lives—after all, their grandmother is still the Queen of England!)

## Q: Does the Queen pay taxes?

A: Yes, since 1992, the Queen has paid 42 percent income tax and capital gains tax just as any high-earning UK taxpayer is required to do.

## Q: If Parliament runs the country, what does the Queen actually do?

A : The UK is a constitutional monarchy. This means that while the Queen is "Head of State" she does not directly rule the country; rather she symbolically appoints the government, which the people of the United Kingdom have democratically elected. Publically, the Queen must remain strictly neutral when it comes to political matters, and she is not able to vote. However, the Queen has hugely important ceremonial roles within the government and retains the right to meet with the prime minister on a regular basis. (In the course of her reign, the present Queen has privately counseled thirteen prime ministers in total.) While the Queen can privately advise, warn, or encourage the prime minister, she cannot make or pass legislation.

Like the American President, the Queen is Head of the Armed Forces. (She also happens to be the wife, mother, and grandmother of those who have served or are currently serving in the Armed Forces. Not all American presidents can say that!) The Queen is also the only person who can formally declare war and peace.

Ultimately, the Queen provides a focus for British national identity, unity, and pride and gives the country a sense of stability and continuity. There is actually a massive (albeit unconscious) comfort that comes with having one easily recognized family dynasty. Even Americans instinctively veer toward familiar dynasties when choosing their leaders. Think about it: the Adamses, the Roosevelts, the Kennedys—and even quite recently, with the Bushes and the Clintons, for a while it seemed that we couldn't think beyond more than two families when it came to selecting our president! The Brits never have this problem. Their beloved Queen is always there in the background—which means they usually vote for politicians based on merit, rather than a familiar family name.

## Q: Why are Roman Catholics excluded from the line of succession?

A: When he decided to divorce Catherine of Aragon in 1534, King Henry VIII broke all ties with Rome and pronounced himself Head of the Church of England.* As a result, every sovereign since Queen Elizabeth I has held the title "Defender of the Faith and Supreme Governor of the Church of England"—which means all those in the line of succession must be Protestants. However, Prince Charles has made it clear that when he becomes king he will take the title "Defender of Faith" instead of "Defender of *the* Faith" in order to formally promote tolerance and understanding of all other faiths and religions. (Go, Charles!) The Act of Settlement was amended in 2012 so that heirs to the throne could *marry* Cath-

---

* Read *The Other Boleyn Girl* (the book by Philippa Gregory, not the movie!) for the full sex-infused royal drama that led to the creation of the Church of England.

olics, but the ban on Catholics becoming sovereign remains in place.

## Q: Why did King Edward VIII have to give up the throne in order to marry American socialite Wallis Simpson?

A: The Royal Marriages Act of 1772 requires members of the Royal Family to obtain permission from the sovereign in order to marry. It was common knowledge that Prince Edward's father, King George V, did not approve of Wallis as a match for Edward and repeatedly refused to meet her. This had nothing to do with the fact that Wallis was American; it had to do with the fact she was twice *divorced*—a concept that was considered incredibly scandalous at the time. Furthermore, if Edward married Wallis he would be her *third* husband—even more scandalous! Upon the death of King George V in 1936, the UK government strongly advised Edward not to marry Wallis, warning him that he would risk upsetting not only the country but the entire Commonwealth. Rather than cause a constitutional crisis, Edward chose to abdicate because, as he told the nation, "I have found it impossible . . . to discharge my duties as king . . . without the help and support of the woman I love."

Nearly seventy years later, Queen Elizabeth II gave her permission for Prince Charles to marry divorcée Camilla Parker Bowles, which goes to show just how much times have changed. If Wallis had been around today, England could very well have had an American Queen . . .

## RECOMMENDED READING:

### Debrett's Correct Form

Indispensable guidance on the notoriously complex system of British titles and forms of address.

### Debrett's Peerage and Baronetage

Contains the genealogical details of every British duke, marquess, viscount, earl, baron, and baronet, together with all the living members of their families in the male line. (A great place to search for possible titled husbands.)

### The Court Circular

The authoritative record of official duties undertaken by senior members of the Royal Family. An account of the previous day's royal engagements is printed daily in the *Times*, the *Telegraph*, and the *Scotsman* and is also available online. Details include places visited in the UK and overseas, duties undertaken, royal audiences, meetings held, ceremonies attended, and official royal appointments. www .royal.gov.uk/LatestNewsandDiary/CourtCircular/Todaysevents .aspx

# FIVE

# How to Catch an Englishman

## (With or Without a Title)

*He had one of those English faces*
*That always were and will always be*
*Found in the cream of English places*
—FROM THE WHITE CLIFFS BY ALICE DUER MILLER

All any girl needs to do is look at Hollywood to see how devastatingly attractive British boys can be. (Come on, don't deny that visions of Robert Pattinson, Jim Sturgess, Henry Cavill, Orlando Bloom, Jude Law, Colin Firth, Matthew McFadyen, Eddie Redmayne, Damian Lewis, Nicholas Hoult, Andrew Garfield, Toby Hemmingway, Max Irons, Sam Claflin, Jamie Bell, Christian Bale, Paul Bettany, Joseph Fiennes, Ralph Fiennes, Cillian Murphy, Chiwetel Ejiofor, Rufus Sewell, Jack Davenport, Jack

Huston, Daniel Craig, Daniel Radcliffe, Rupert Grint, Rupert Everett, Rupert Friend, and Hugh Dancy and/or Hugh Grant haven't danced in your head at least once, if not a million times.)

Who cares if they're all named Jack, Daniel, Rupert, or Hugh? Have you heard their accents? Have you seen their cheekbones? Enough said.

## Your Crush Is Nothing New

*Marrying American girls . . . was something*
*an Englishman had to reckon with, like the railway,*
*the telegraph, the discovery of dynamite . . . it was*
*one of the complications of modern life.*
—HENRY JAMES

American girls lusting after British men is nothing new— Anglophile crushes like yours and mine have been going on for well over a century.

During the Gilded Age (1870–1890), America was blessed with a period of rapid economic growth—industries were thriving, new money was flooding in from all directions, and new American heiresses were popping up all over the place. Even so, the snobby old-money families of Manhattan were not happy with this sudden influx of nouveau riche girls flirting with their sons, and as a result, many ballroom doors were slammed in these girls' faces. But these wealthy young women were not daunted. They'd heard that English society was much easier to crack than New York society, so they simply packed up their best ball gowns and sailed off to London—more than ready to continue their husband hunt on the other side of the pond.

These American girls took London by storm. Just like today, they were better dressed and better groomed than their English counterparts—and they loved to shop. (It was not uncommon for American girls to order at least ninety dresses per season!) Many members of the English aristocracy were shocked by this conspicuous display of American beauty; scandalized by the girls' free-spirited natures, easygoing manners, and "modern" worldviews (not to mention a bit shaken up by the fact that American girls dared to wear diamonds in the daytime)—but luckily, their eligible British sons didn't seem to mind. In fact, the Englishmen loved it.

For both parties, it was a match made in heaven. The American girls had good looks and big bucks; the British boys had debts, but they also had titles. Everyone was happy. The American girl got her castle—and with her dowry, the British boy could finally afford to keep it standing.

The phenomenon of American women pursuing upper-class English husbands was popularly immortalized in the novels of Henry James and Edith Wharton (both of whom you should read). And by 1936, Americans had managed to completely infiltrate the heart of London's social elite—the young Prince of Wales was constantly found in their carefree, extravagant company— and eventually fell in love with one himself—ultimately forsaking the throne for her! (See "American Beauty," page 79.)

The Prince of Wales's infamous paramour was the American Wallis Simpson. Personally, I love how the immaculately dressed Wallis used to host lavish London luncheons where she proudly served American club sandwiches and beer—and how the aristocratic Brits found this unassuming quirkiness to be utterly, utterly charming. Still, Wallis and her plucky American pals managed to alarm the stuffier members of the Court (which was most of them).

Aside from the indomitable Wallis, the most famous American

women married to British noblemen are Jennie Jerome, the mother of Sir Winston Churchill, and Consuelo Vanderbilt (second cousin to mother of reporter Anderson Cooper, Gloria Vanderbilt), who married the Duke of Marlborough.

Even our beloved Princess Diana had an American great-grandmother—one Frances Ellen Work. Frances married The Hon. James Roche, who later became the 3rd Baron Fermoy. Their son Edmund married Diana's grandmother Ruth Gill, whose daughter Frances went on to marry the 8th Earl Spencer, Diana's father. So basically if it wasn't for a feisty American girl named Frances, who crossed the pond in search of an English husband, Prince William and Prince Harry wouldn't be here. (Dear Kate, you're welcome.)

But a hundred years ago, an American girl often paid a high price for her swanky aristocratic title. Many found themselves living in huge, crumbling castles deep in the English countryside, with no heating apart from open fires and, even worse, no running water. Luckily, English stately homes have improved a bit since then*— so don't let that deter you from your transatlantic objective.

And one more thing—please don't let a lack of massive family inheritance stop you from going after your man. In the wise words of one Dowager Duchess of Roxburghe, let us remember that "money isn't everything to an Englishman. There are other considerations when he marries; for instance, fondness for the girl."

Indeed.

That said, don't let *anyone* accuse you of gold-digging. You're a big girl. No one needs to tell you that palaces and jewels can come

---

* Nevertheless, I actually know an American woman who refuses to stay in any Englishman's country house unless she has physical proof that there is central heating and a decent coffee machine.

and go, and that most aristocratic families are not nearly as wealthy as they seem (many have had to sell off their houses, their furniture, and their art collections—and have essentially lost everything but their titles). I know that, like all girls with a fairy-tale dream, your driving force isn't money—it's *love*!

In this day and age (especially if you call yourself a feminist), it can be hard to admit that you believe in the old-fashioned fairy-tale dream of true love. Modern women aren't supposed to want that. We're not supposed to want to fall in love with a prince or duke. It's much trendier, much more "progressive" for twenty-first-century women to pretend we don't have these dreams. But I'm afraid that doesn't make them go away.

In reality, setting your sights on finding "a prince" (real or conceptual) is actually making a very strong statement about your own self-worth. You *know* you deserve the best and see no reason why you shouldn't aim for the stars.

I get that. You get that. (And you better believe that one Frances Ellen Work gets that.) Who cares if no one else does?

So now that you're happily living and working in London—and know exactly what to wear, what to do, and what to say in the company of polite society (as well as what *not* to)—it is time to stop swooning and go after the Englishman of your dreams. If those fearless American girls could do it all those years ago, then you can certainly do it today.

So let's start with the Holy Grail:

# HRH Prince Henry (Harry) of Wales

I admit it. I'll admit it to you and I'll admit it to anyone who asks: I once harbored a sincere desire to be a princess. But to achieve this career goal, I had to marry a prince, and since my country was (and is) severely lacking in this department, right after college I moved to England and commenced my search. The royal marriage didn't work out, but I ended up writing a rather amusing memoir about crossing the ocean to pursue this quirky childhood dream. And since its publication, lots of people have pronounced me certifiably insane. I expected that. But something else happened that I did not expect. I have been overwhelmed with letters and emails from

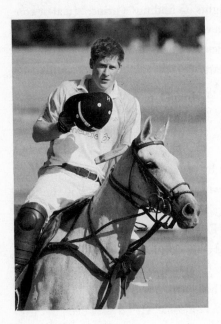

young women all around the world who also want to be a princess (or marry an English aristocrat)—and who, until they read my book, thought they were the only ones in the entire universe who felt that way.

A lot of the girls who write to me have their hearts set on Prince Harry—and who can blame them? He's *hot*. Not to mention that third* in line to the British throne is nothing to sniff at. Harry

---

* At least until William and Kate reproduce.

may never inherit a kingdom, but without all that responsibility, he is able (and clearly willing) to have a lot more fun. William has a huge sense of duty, but Harry has this incredible, laid-back magnetism and that super-sexy mischievous grin. And when it comes to love, something tells me this rowdy redhead has plans to ditch tradition and follow his heart. Royal or no royal, what right-minded girl wouldn't go after him?

Many accuse these "Harry Hunting" girls of being stalkers, gold-diggers, or just plain delusional. But I've met a lot of them and they are nothing of the sort. They are normal American girls who just happen to have big fairy-tale dreams. Most are in London on college exchange programs and find England, with its plethora of palaces and its living, breathing Royal Family, to be absolutely magical. They go to nightclubs like any student would; they attend quintessentially English events like polo and rugby, just like anyone enjoying the UK for the first time might do. And yes, like all single girls in the capital, they keep their eyes open for their personal prince charming. My advice to them is this: Godspeed.

If you believe in your heart that you are worthy of a prince, then don't let anyone tell you otherwise.

## Harry Hunting

Only a few years ago, Prince William was indisputably the world's favorite royal heartthrob. I'll never forget the photo taken during his first year at St. Andrews: His navy sweater hung perfectly off his swimmer's physique, his cheeks had color, his head had hair, and he looked breathtakingly handsome. (If I'd only been but five years younger!)

Yet in recent years, I'm afraid William's premature baldness and knockout wife have removed him from the most eligible prince position. No one is quite sure when it happened, but young Harry surprised us all when he suddenly emerged as the hottest prince in the land. (Here's to you, Harry. We didn't see it coming.)

Looking at Harry, it's hard not to think of his legendary mother—Diana, Princess of Wales—and as the years go by, it's clear that Harry has inherited her caring, empathetic nature. Harry has often declared his determination to honor his mother's memory by embracing charity work that helps the disadvantaged: "I want to carry on the things she didn't quite finish," he says. (Have you gone weak at the knees yet?)

When not dispatched on a courageous military mission, our handsome soldier is most likely to be found playing polo and clubbing till dawn, but if you are serious about winning his heart, you might want to get involved with one of his charities. Maybe throw a charity fund-raiser and invite him? Crazier things have happened.

PRINCE HARRY'S CHARITIES:

*Sentebale: The Princes' Fund for Lesotho.* Founded by Prince Harry and Prince Seeiso of Lesotho in response to the plight of Lesotho's AIDS orphans and vulnerable children. www .sentebale.org

*Walking with the Wounded.* Funds further education for seriously injured Armed Forces personnel, helping them rebuild their lives and return to a work. Harry is a patron and recently joined a team of disabled servicemen as they trekked through the Arctic in aide of this charity. http://walkingwiththewounded .org.uk

*WellChild.* Helps sick children and their families across the UK. Prince Harry is a patron and can often be seen chatting and joking with the children. www.wellchild.org.uk

*MapAction.* Creates maps during natural disasters to highlight where medical attention is most needed. Prince Harry is a patron and is looking forward to training with them. www.mapaction.org/about.html

*Henry van Straubenzee Memorial Fund.* Aims to lift Ugandan children out of poverty through education. (Henry van Straubenzee, a schoolmate and close friend of Prince Harry, was killed in a car crash in 2002.) Princes William and Harry are joint patrons. www.henryvanstraubenzeemf.org.uk

*Absolute Return for Kids (ARK).* Delivers programs in the areas of health, education, and child protection across the globe. www.arkonline.org

*Help for Heroes.* A charity formed to help those who have been wounded in Britain's current conflicts. www.helpforheroes.org.uk

*Dolen Cymru.* Creates life-changing links between Wales and Lesotho in the fields of education, health, and civil society. Prince Harry is a patron. www.dolencymru.org

*The Prince's Rainforests Project.* Founded by his father, The Prince of Wales, to discourage deforestation rates and promote the link between rain forests and climate change. Princes William and Harry appeared alongside their father and an animated frog in a recent public awareness film. www.rainforestsos.org

*Diana, Princess of Wales Memorial Fund.* Established in September 1997 to continue his mother's humanitarian work throughout the world. www.theworkcontinues.org

For more information on Prince Harry's philanthropic engagements, write to: The Foundation of Prince William and Prince Harry, St James's Palace, London, SW1A 1BS, United Kingdom.

In the 1880s, competition for the young Prince of Wales's* affection was so fierce that American girls would pay to have themselves professionally photographed and then allow their photos to be displayed in shop windows all around London. You have to give them credit for trying, but I don't think it's necessary for you to go to such lengths. Instead, try to follow these regal rules . . .

GOLDEN RULES FOR HARRY HUNTERS:

- Be as discreet as possible. Don't tell everyone in the nightclub that you're looking for Prince Harry because you plan on falling in love and bearing his children (even if you believe this to be true).

- Dress appropriately (not too trendy, not too trashy). See Chapter 3.

- Smile demurely and say as little as possible. (For inspiration, watch the ball scene in *My Fair Lady*.)

---

* Edward, Prince of Wales (crowned King Edward V in 1910).

- Try not to get nervous. (Don't forget that royal guys can be just as hopeless as any other guy.)

- Too much deference can cause embarrassment or draw unwanted attention—so when in doubt, stay calm, and take the lead from his friends.

- Frequent the following night spots as often as possible (ideally on a Monday or Tuesday night): Public, Mahiki, Boujis, and The Box. (See "London Nightclubs," page 132.)

- Learn to love polo and rugby. If Harry's not playing one, he's watching the other.

- Hang out in the village of Tetbury—you never know if Harry is home from a military mission and stopping by Highgrove to visit his dad.

- Read all you can about the House of Windsor. Make sure you know who's who, how everyone is related, their official duties, and the charities they support. (*Tatler*, *Hello*, and *Vanity Fair* can often be better and more up-to-date sources of information than magazines like *Royalty* and *Majesty*.)

- Study up on royal history. If you don't know that Queen Victoria is Harry's great-great-great-great-grandmother then you're probably not going to fit into his family that well.

- Don't be discouraged if people make fun of you or call you crazy—there is nothing more honorable than following your heart.

- Don't be discouraged if people tell you that meeting Harry is unrealistic. Winning *American Idol* is also pretty unrealistic—

but if you believe something is your destiny, don't let anyone stop you from trying.

# Planning Your Pursuit

*Every American girl is entitled to have twelve
young men devoted to her. They remain her slaves
and she rules them with charming nonchalance.*
—Oscar Wilde

Once you arrive in London, one of the first things you'll notice is that Prince Harry–type Englishmen with Hugh Grant accents are few and far between. The movies make it look like they are swarming the streets, but the reality is that they practically belong on some sort of endangered species list.

But don't fret. The good news is that although this particular species of Englishman makes up *less than 4 percent* of the entire UK population, they are not extinct. You just have to know where to find them. The junior royals are spotted out and about in London all the time—as are their devastatingly attractive friends that I like to call the "Castle Crew" (aka cute British boys, usually Eton or Harrow alumni, whose families tend to own rather large stately homes). Although there is no question that the Castle Crew is an increasingly threatened species and the enchanted world these boys inhabit is very, very small— if you get in, you're likely to stay in.

Follow my advice, and soon you'll be dancing with guys that dance with girls that dance with Prince Harry. (And who knows? After a few secret smiles, some careful eye contact, a light touch of the arm, and a bit of teasing conversation . . . you just might need to be referring to visa option #7.

HOW TO SPOT A MEMBER OF THE CASTLE CREW:*

- plummy, cut-glass accent (this one is nonnegotiable!)

- hyphenated last name (or "double-barreled surname")

- refers to his friends (both male and female) by their last names, or diminutives thereof

- bottomless well of self-confidence

- signs of chivalry, gallantry, and manners (He leaps to his feet when a woman enters the room and every time she leaves the table. He opens doors, pays for drinks, and offers his jacket to girls if the night is chilly.)

- strong sense of duty to Queen and country

If the music is too loud to hear him properly, look for at least two or more of the following:

- rosy cheeks

- disheveled hair (that tends to rise into little cute wings behind his ears)

- rowing and/or rugby muscles

- gold signet ring (worn on the pinky finger)—make sure it's bearing a family crest; otherwise steer clear

---

* Also derogatorily known as "Sloane Rangers," "Toffs," "Hooray Henry's," "Ra-Ra-Rupert's," "Chinless Wonders," "Tim-Nice-But-Dim's," "Fops," or quite simply "Yah's"—all referring to the stereotype of a young upper- or upper-middle-class privately educated Englishman.

- pastel-colored shirts (never white) rolled-up below the elbow (never above)

- suede loafers

Always find out where he went to boarding school—this is a lot more telling than where he went to university.* (Bizarrely, private-run schools that charge tuition are called "public schools" in the UK.) Most Castle Crew boys will have boarded from the age of seven at one of the following:

Ampleforth

Bedford

Charterhouse

Eton†

Fettes

Gordonstoun‡

---

* It is interesting to note that even though less than 4 percent of the UK male population went to a private boarding school, graduates of these schools make up 75 percent of UK judges, 70 percent of UK finance directors, 45 percent of UK top civil servants, and 32 percent of British MPs.

† Old Etonians include: Prince William, Prince Harry, Earl Spencer, George Orwell, Ian Fleming (creator of James Bond), Hugh Laurie, Eddie Redmayne, Bear Grylls, Damian Lewis, London Mayor Boris Johnson, and nineteen British prime ministers, including David Cameron. The school uniform consists of white tie, morning coat, and pinstripe trousers.

‡ Old Gordonstounians include The Duke of Edinburgh, Prince Charles, Prince Andrew, Prince Edward, and Princess Anne's children, Peter and Zara.

Hailbury

Harrow*

Marlborough

Milton Abbey

Oundle

Radley

Rugby

St. Paul's

Shiplake

Stowe†

Tonbridge

Uppingham

Wellington

Westminster

Winchester‡

---

* Famous old Harrovians include seven British prime ministers (most notably Winston Churchill), King Hussein of Jordan, James Blunt, and Cary Elwes (the prince in the movie *The Princess Bride*).

† Alma mater of Henry Cavill; alumni are known as "Old Stoics."

‡ Winchester was founded in 1382—making it the oldest "public" school in the world. Because the school was founded by William of Wykeham, alumni (which include the likes of Hugh Dancy) are known as "Old Wykehamists."

*Warning:* British men in this strata of society tend not to wear wedding bands. Prince William doesn't. My husband doesn't. If they do wear a ring, it is their family signet ring, but as a general rule these particular Englishmen don't believe in jewelry of any kind. Watches and cuff links are the only exceptions.

So now that we've established our regal prey, let us commence our hunt . . .

# Regal Hunting Ground #1: London Nightclubs

## When to Go

The Castle Crew tend to have flexible working hours (jobs are considered as gratuitous as new clothes) and prefer to avoid the masses, so you have the best chance of spotting them out and about on Monday or Tuesday nights.

## What to Wear

Smart and sexy is the order of the day. Go for a cute dress, great shoes, and fantastically blown-out hair.

## Faux Pas

Desperation (declaring you "came all the way over from America to get into this club" is unlikely to get you any VIP treatment); acknowledging anyone famous; showing up with a large, co-ed group.

# Best Flirting Spot

Any dark corner will do.

You are categorically not going to find the Castle Crew anywhere in Leicester Square or in any American-themed sports bar. Instead, get yourself on the following guest lists:

### *Boujis*, 42 Thurloe Street, London SW7

An intimate basement club with low ceilings, dark lighting, and secluded banquettes. Champagne only comes vintage and the vodka is quadruple distilled.

**Who goes:** Prince Harry, Orlando Bloom, Leonardo DiCaprio, Lord Freddy Windsor, Lady Gabriella Windsor, and the Duke and Duchess of Cambridge (though, to be fair, Kate and Will have been asked by the Queen to spend less time clubbing and more time doing newlywed stuff in Wales).

**What to drink:** The "crack baby"—a shot-sized mix of vodka and champagne.

Membership is approximately $825 a year and the waiting list is approximately one year.

### *Mahiki*, 1 Dover Street, London W1S

My personal favorite. Think bamboo beach bars, palm fronds, exotic flowers, and coconuts cocktails. The royals are regulars at this Hawaiian hideaway, and I can see why.

**Who goes:** Prince Harry, William and Kate, Zara Phillips, Princess Beatrice, Princess Eugenie.

**What to drink:** The Mahiki Treasure Chest—a mix of Mahiki beer, brandy, peach liqueur, lime, and sugar, all topped with a bottle of Moët. The drink is served in an actual treasure chest, with eight straws.

**Tip:** Go early (like 5:30 p.m.) and stay all night. Entry is free before 9 p.m.

### *PUBLIC,* 533 King's Road, London SW3

Opened by the young Guy Pelly (master of royal revels and Harry and William's party companion of choice), this elite nightclub was rumored to be the venue of William's secret bachelor party. The club's name is an ironic play on "public school" (which is confusingly what the Brits call private school). Situated in an old antiques warehouse, PUBLIC managed to bring an edgy New York/East London vibe straight to the heart of Chelsea. You'll find exposed brick walls, iron beams, industrial lighting, and red leather seating, as well as a huge dance floor, life-sized carousel horses, and a dress-up corner and photo booth (because, as you will soon find out, these silly Brits can't get enough of "fancy dress"!). The VIP area is called the "sweet room" and is decorated like an old-fashioned candy store.

**Who goes:** Prince Harry, Princess Eugenie, Princess Beatrice, James Blunt.

**What to drink:** The Jägerbomb Mousetrap; the actual board game is served to your table and the toy mousetrap eventually knocks shots of Jägermeister into your glass.

PUBLIC is guest list only (and only for those who are twenty-one and over), so your best bet is to book a table in advance.

### *Kitts,* 7–12 Sloane Square, London SW3

This club's tagline is: "All is not what it seems on Sloane Square." The place is named after the Caribbean island of St. Kitts; expect a vibrant party spirit, sparkling dance floor, luxurious booths, and rum-based cocktails.

**Who goes:** Kate Middleton chose Kitts for her twenty-fifth birthday party.

**What to order:** The signature bar snack is French fries with caviar.

### *The Box*, 12 Walkers Court, London W1F

The Box is an infamous and utterly risqué club that was a cult hit in Manhattan before opening in London. The Box offers everything from vaudeville to burlesque and boasts the strangest and naughtiest cabaret acts imaginable, almost all of which involve some degree of nudity. The general atmosphere is one of slightly controlled debauchery.

**Who goes:** Hugh Grant, the roguish Prince Harry and his plucky cousins Princesses Beatrice and Eugenie.

**What to drink:** The Dirty Lady—a mixture of gin and Moët.

Doors open at 11 p.m., shows start at approximately 1 a.m. Cameras, BlackBerrys, and phones are prohibited.

### *Beaufort House*, 354 King's Road, London SW3

Beaufort House has three floors, two cocktails bars, a champagne bar, and a restaurant.

**Who goes:** Princes Harry, Zara Phillips, the England Rugby team (think sturdy, stocky heartthrobs with big smiles and even bigger thigh muscles).

**What to drink:** The spiced pear mojito.

Membership is $650 a year, and you must be recommended by two existing members. However, an existing member can sign you in as a guest.

### *Raffles*, 287 King's Road, London SW3

This notorious members club began its glamorous life in 1967 and is named after the nineteenth-century colonial mogul Sir Thomas Stamford Raffles. Strict doormen keep the riffraff out.

**Who goes:** Prince Harry, the Duke and Duchess of Cambridge, Rosamund Pike, Keira Knightley.

Membership is approximately $815 per year.

### *Whiskey Mist*, 35 Hertford Street, London W1J

Whiskey Mist is derived from the name of Queen Victoria's favorite stag, which she reportedly enjoyed watching from her window at Balmoral, while sipping a snifter of whiskey. Naturally, whiskey features strongly on the menu, and you can even purchase impromptu shooting trips in the Scottish Highlands. (After a night out at Whiskey Mist, you never know where you might end up.)

**Who goes:** Princes William and Harry; Princesses Beatrice and Eugenie have even been made to queue at this über hotspot, located beneath the Park Lane Hilton.

**What to drink:** The Tree of Life—a vodka and champagne cocktail, which is served in a two-handled silver quaich (a Victorian victory cup) engraved with the name of the buyer. (Warning: This cocktail costs $1,140.)

**Tip:** Take the elevator (or "lift") to the top floor of the building for one of the best views of London.

This is a slightly older crowd than Mahiki. Membership is approximately $570 per year.

### *Eighty Six*, 86 Fulham Rd, London SW3

A swanky new bar and restaurant occupying a grand Georgian town house, run by Brit entrepreneurs George Adams and Charlie

Kearns, who also run the infamous Coco Club in Verbier. (See "Sailing and Skiing Holidays," page 161.) Think mosaic floors, velvet sofas, gold paneling, and antique mirrors.

**Who goes:** Kate Middleton celebrated her twenty-ninth birthday here.

**What to order:** Lobster on toast.

### *The Arts Club*, 40 Dover Street, London, W1S

Cofounded by Charles Dickens in 1838, this Mayfair town house boasts a bistro, brasserie, conservatory, drawing room, library, and nightclub and plays host to a frivolous, fashionable crowd. The club's contemporary art collection is just as impressive as the people-watching.

**Who goes:** Prince Harry, The Crown Prince and Crown Princess of Greece, Gwyneth Paltrow, Thandie Newton, the Red Hot Chili Peppers.

Membership is approximately $2300 per year (or $1175 if you are under 30). New members must be proposed and seconded by existing members of the club.

### *Brompton Club*, 92b Old Brompton Road, London SW7

Another discreet watering hole for the famous and formidable, the Brompton Club is a private members restaurant and nightclub. With the look and feel of a 1920s supper club (think dark wood and emerald green wallpaper), the venue boasts two opulent bars and a fine dining area that later transforms into a dance floor.

**Who goes:** Prince Harry, Chelsy Davy, Princess Eugenie, and Jason Lewis (aka Smith Jarrod from *Sex and the City)*

It is nearly impossible to enter this impenetrable fortress unless it is on the arm of one of its fashionable members.

### *Annabel's*, 4 Berkley Square, London W15

A London institution that has been going on since 1963, Annabel's is the only place to party with the young, the old, the rich, and the beautiful.

**Who goes:** Hugh Grant himself was spotted here during his courtship with Jemima Khan—which makes sense since this infamous Mayfair club was named after her mother, Lady Annabel Goldsmith. If you're lucky, you'll run into the dreamy Zac Goldsmith, one of the handsomer new Members of Parliament. (Many say he will be prime minister in our lifetime—I've met him and can't help but agree.)

You must be the guest of a member to enter.

### *151*, 151 King's Rd, London SW3

AKA "one-five-dive." This is one of the most hilarious hunting grounds in existence. It hasn't been refurbished in decades, but its old school charm remains and it's guaranteed to be full of good-looking, well-bred Englishmen of all ages. If you can look beyond the frayed decor, it's almost impossible not to have a good time. (Thankfully, there is no guest list.)

**TOP TIP:**

You might want to consider joining Champagne for Life. Exclusively for women, this membership is available as a sleek business card or iPhone App. Members can enjoy a complimentary glass of champagne at a number of prestigious venues in London (and around the world) for life! Most importantly, you will receive complimentary entry to private members clubs (including royal favorites Boujis, Beauford House, Kitts, and Eighty Six), priority queuing, and invitations to exclusive events. It's not cheap, but if you already spend £10 pounds a week at swanky London bars, membership will have paid for itself in less than a year. www .champagneforlife.com

# Regal Hunting Ground #2:
# London Pubs

Only a few years ago, most pubs in London were pretty unpleasant places filled with tacky game machines, beer-soaked carpeting, microwaved food, and a somewhat unsavory clientele. However, things have changed drastically since the smoking ban kicked in, and there are a few absolute gems that are worth going out of your way for.

On my secret preferred pub list you'll find nothing but warm and cozy lighting, fashionable (and clean) furniture, superior food and wine, and most of all, plenty of gorgeous and gregarious, well-spoken Englishmen. When in doubt order wine, gin and tonic, or Pimm's (see what not to order on the next page), and rather than tip for stellar service, it is customary to buy the barman a drink.* Please note that last orders are taken at 11 p.m. and that dogs are almost always allowed. Don't be shocked if you see children in the pub—during the day, Brits consider pubs to be "family" destinations.

---

* Needless to say, most London bar staff are not sober. The upside to this is you can often convince them to give a cute American girl a free shot.

- *The White Horse*, Parsons Green, SW6 (aka "the Sloaney Pony"—it has a ludicrously popular outdoor terrace that spills onto the green; wonderfully flirty and social on a summer afternoon)

- *The Admiral Codrington*, Mossop Street, SW3 (*love* this place)

- *The Sands End*, Stephendale Road, SW6 (excellent for sightings of Prince Harry)

- *The Pig's Ear*, Old Church Street, SW3 (a known favorite of Prince William)

- *The Ship*, Wandsworth Bridge Road, SW18 (popular with the rugby crowd and all the Queen's grandchildren)

- *Aragon House*, New Kings Road, SW6

- *The Builders Arms*, Britten Street, SW3

- *The Windsor Castle*, Campden Hill Road, W8

- *The Phoenix*, Smith Street, SW3

- *The Punchbowl*, Farm Street, W1J (owned by Madonna's ex-husband Guy Ritchie)

- *The Grenadier*, Wilton Row, SW1

DRINKS THAT NICE PUB-GOING GIRLS SHOULD AVOID:

- Pints of anything, including cider (I know it tastes like apple juice, but you must refrain.)

- Bacardi Breezers or any sweet, pastel-colored "alco-pop"

- Shots of Aftershock (If you *must* do shots, go with something classic and slightly less vulgar, like vodka or tequila.)

- Creamy cocktails

# Regal Hunting Ground #3:
# Certain UK Universities

*The exquisite art of idleness is one of the*
*most important things that any university can teach.*
—OSCAR WILDE

When Rupert first invited me to visit him at his university, I was astounded. Don't get me wrong, I partied a lot during my student days in America. In fact it was not uncommon for me to attend college parties at least five days a week.

But British students? They put me to shame. There are three major reasons for this. The first is that the drinking age in the UK is eighteen, so all colleges have their own *university-sponsored* pubs and bars. The second is that freshman year grades don't count. That's right. They simply *don't count*. So your first year of college is genuinely one giant party partly subsidized by the UK government. The third reason is there are no GPAs,* only year-end exams—so

---

* You emerge from your stint at university with one of the following: 1st class degree (A average), 2:1 (B average), 2:2 (C average), or 3rd class degree (D average). Personally, I've never met anyone that graduated with anything other than 2:1, so I'm not quite sure how British employers differentiate among applicants.

you often have absolutely no course work to do until the end of the term, which is when you start cramming.

Still, while academia did not seem to be at the forefront of UK campus life, the student social scene was fantastic. The more time I spent with the Bright Young Things, the more I realized the social maturity of these British college kids greatly surpassed American students of the same age. Their parties weren't full of the juvenile fraternity/sorority antics I was used to; their bashes were straight out of Oscar Wilde. As young twenty-somethings, they seemed to be in total denial that they were living in a new millennium, and coped by pretending to be mini nineteenth-century adults. Bearing in mind that I've always pretended to be exactly the same thing, I loved every second of it.

## Where to Go

St. Andrews, Oxford, Cambridge, Bristol, Exeter, Durham, Edinburgh, Oxford Brookes, University of West England, and the Royal Agricultural College. As mentioned previously, when scouting student territories, avoid London.

## What to Expect

Raucous private house parties, university bars (avoid local ones!), minor alcohol poisoning, and *a lot* of kissing*—it is not uncommon for these boys to make out with three or more girls in a single evening.

---

* I actually know of one UK university that permanently canceled their annual Valentine's Day party due to constant outbreaks of mono (or "glandular fever").

## What to Wear

(Unless it's fancy dress) designer jeans, tasteful yet dazzling party tops with a hint of cleavage, high heels, a warm but flattering coat for walking home at night when you can't find a taxi.

## What to Drink

At parties? Whatever's on offer. (Homemade sangria and cheap white wine are the usual suspects.)
At bars? Gin and tonic.

## Best Flirting Spot

Anywhere and everywhere.

## Faux Pas

Showing any regard for grades, exams, or academic standing. (With this crowd, it's considered bad manners to be clever or too hardworking. It implies that your family's history and status aren't enough to get you by in life.)

## Top Tip

Make sure your lipstick isn't smudged.

## Best Student Hangover Cure

A "bacon and butter butty" (aka a "bacon and butter sandwich"). My first reaction when I was offered one of these was that I'd never heard of anything that sounded less healthy—but they are delicious and they do the trick.

---

## Binge Drinking

Student binge drinking is currently considered to be a huge problem among US universities, but oddly, it's not considered to be a problem at all in the UK. One journalist, intrigued by this anomaly, did some research into how the US and UK officially defined student "binge drinking" and unearthed some very entertaining results:

- *American definition*: "five beers in one sitting for a male, or four for a female."
- *British definition*: "an extended period of time, lasting *at least two days*, during which a student repeatedly becomes intoxicated and gives up his or her usual activities and obligations in order to become intoxicated."

Hassinger, Kris. "Binge drinking problem exaggerated," *Collegiate Times.com*, November 2003.

---

HOW TO BE A GRACEFUL DRUNK:

- Don't go beyond the light-headed, cheeks-tingling, hugging-everyone-you-know phase—throwing up and passing out is not attractive. Or safe.

- Know your limit. (Between the ages of eighteen and twenty-six, my limit was exactly seven drinks per evening; I regret to report that now it's exactly 1.5.)

❧ Don't drink on an empty stomach!

❧ No matter how fast the drinks are flowing, duck into the loo occasionally to check your appearance. Powder away the shine, pop in some eye drops, reapply your lipstick, and smooth your hair. Because looking sober is the next best thing to being sober.

❧ Never fall out of the club/pub into the first mini cab you see (it's dangerous, not to mention getting into a stranger's car while under the influence is everything your mother told you not to do). Always go home in a licensed black cab.

❧ Before you go to bed, eat a piece of toast, drink two (if not three) glasses of water, and pop a pair of pills for your head. (FYI: Nurofen = Ibuprofen; Paracetmol = Tylenol.)

❧ In the morning, drink coffee and wear your best Jackie O sunglasses.

# Parable #3

Whenever I went out for drinks with a group of British friends, students, or coworkers, someone would kindly offer to buy me a gin and tonic, so I'd thank them profusely and graciously accept. Inevitably, before my drink was halfway finished, someone else would offer to buy me a drink, and again, I'd thank them for the kindness and happily accept. Afterward, I usually had to go meet my gay best friend for dinner or head across town for another puzzling "date" with a English boy, so I'd thank them again, say good-bye to everyone, and be on my way.

Little did I know that this was the height of rudeness. Worse than that, it was practically heresy.

In the UK, drinking is done in *rounds*. If you are out socializing with eight people, you are expected to drink *eight* drinks, because every single one of you is expected to buy *a round* of eight drinks. If you have a headache and only feel like drinking one drink or you simply can't afford to buy eight drinks, then apparently you shouldn't be consuming alcohol in public whatsoever.

This isn't just bizarre British drinking etiquette, it's actually some kind of sacred British obligation—and god knows how many Brits I offended before I realized my mistake.

# Regal Hunting Ground #3:
# Sporting Events

In England, there is a well-known saying that everyone loves to repeat: *Football is a gentleman's game played by hooligans, and rugby is a hooligan's game played by gentlemen.*

I can't stress to you how true this is. The most important piece of advice I can give you on this subject of UK sporting events is to avoid football matches (aka soccer games) like the plague.

I realize that compared to the high-impact activity of the NFL, soccer looks positively elegant. Graceful even. And in the US, soccer players tend to reflect this. (In my high school, members of the soccer team were among some of the highest achieving and well-rounded students in the district.)

Yet in England the reverse tends to be true. UK soccer games have a reputation for being filled with spectators that look as though they have done time for assault, and alcohol is not allowed in the stadiums for this very reason. Promise me—steer clear.

But in terms of Hunting Grounds, all is not lost. If you're looking for handsomely rowdy and roguish English boys (that also happen to be true gentlemen), I guarantee you will find them at any:

- *rugby match*
- *cricket match*
- *polo match*
- *tennis match*

It doesn't matter if you don't understand the rules to any of the above. I certainly don't. But I assure you that even if you have no idea what is happening during the game itself, all of these sporting events are splendid social occasions that also happen to be filled with eligible Englishmen. (And if any guy dares to give you trouble about the fact that you possess less than a working knowledge of the above sports, just ask him to explain the Eton Wall Game. That should silence him pretty quickly—as I'm pretty sure that less than 50 percent of the players understand it themselves.)

## Rugby (A Hooligan's Game Played by Gentlemen)

Until rather recently, rugby union players were not allowed to earn any money through sponsorship or advertising (because after all, only the lower classes require an income.)

**Where to go:** Any England or Wales match at Twickenham.

**What to expect:** Mauling, rucking, scrums, and something

quite worryingly called a "blood bin."* But all you really need to know is that rugby players have big sturdy thighs, big muscley shoulders, and (because they refuse to wear protective gear of any kind) they are always getting spectacularly and violently injured.

**What to drink:** Bitter, Lager, or Guinness. Throughout the entire game. No hot dogs or peanuts or Cracker Jack. Just pints and pints and pints of beer. Needless to say, the queue for the ladies loo can be rather lengthy.

**Who goes:** If England or Wales is playing, sightings of Prince Harry, William and Kate, Zara Phillips (her husband, Mike Tindall, is a former England captain), and their Castle Crew friends are regular occurrences.

**Warning:** Every girl I know who is dating a rugby player spends most weekends by his hospital bedside, faithfully tending to his injury of the week.

## Cricket

> *Most of us think life is a game;*
> *the English think cricket is a game.*
> —GEORGES MIKES

Admittedly, the rules of cricket are a minefield if you haven't grown up with them (from what I can tell, one player's sole task is to hold onto his teammate's sweater for safekeeping), but what I love most about cricket is that people dress up for it.

**Where to go:** Lord's Cricket Ground will have a slightly higher

---

* A fifteen-minute time-out for players with visibly bleeding injuries.

caliber of spectator than the Oval. (Although Hugh Grant has been spotted at both.)

**What to wear:** Summery dresses for women, linen suits for men.

**What to expect:** Victorian stands filled with spectators leisurely reading the *Sunday Times*, munching on delicate finger sandwiches, sipping chilled wine and pitchers of Pimm's, and stopping only occasionally to glance at the scoreboard to see how England is progressing. And of course the game pauses at 4 p.m. sharp to allow for afternoon tea. You can see why it's my kind of sport. Believe me, if baseball involved a semiformal dress code and a civilized tea break, I might be more of a fan.

**Best flirting spots:** The Marylebone Cricket Club (MCC) Pavilion; the Eton vs. Harrow match (think of the alumni!).

**How to spot MCC members:** The distinctive gold and red necktie (affectionately referred to as "egg and bacon").

**Faux pas:** Arguing with the umpire (this is a gentleman's game after all).

## Polo

See Chapter 6, "The Season," page 173.

## Tennis

See "Tennis Clubs," p. 150; see also "Wimbledon," page 184.

# Regal Hunting Ground #4:
# Tennis Clubs

*The Queen's Club*, Baron's Court, London,
www.queensclub.co.uk

Featured in the Woody Allen movie *Match Point*, this is one of the most coveted club memberships in the UK. Named after Queen Victoria, The Queen's Club was the first multipurpose sports complex to be built anywhere on earth and is one of the most prestigious tennis clubs in the country, if not the world.

More than anything, this club is known for hosting tournaments of a spin-off game called "racquets"—a game that is only taught at exclusive British boarding schools. Only a dozen or so courts on the planet can even facilitate racquets, and Queen's Club has two of them.

When it comes to sports that I actually, genuinely enjoy watching—this one ranks right behind polo. The game moves so fast and the players move with such amazing, inhuman skill my heart actually pumps with excitement. (Though I'm sure the champagne helps.)

Did I mention that Queen's also happens to have a marvelous bar? And some really cute semiprofessional players whom I may or may not have snogged in my youth? Highly, highly recommended.

*The Hurlingham Club*, Putney Bridge, London
www.hurlinghamclub.org.uk

With a membership waiting list of sixteen years(!), this striking Georgian clubhouse is set on two acres of magnificently manicured grounds alongside the River Thames. When I first moved to London, a lovely floppy-haired Englishman (whom I happened to meet at The Queen's Club) took me on a date to this quintessentially English paradise, and as I held his hand and entered a world of timeless elegance, I felt like Dorothy in *The Wizard of Oz* as she entered Munchkinland—it was that magical, and that unexpected.

Up until World War II, the club hosted all major polo events for the British Empire. Today at the Hurlingham you can watch polo, play tennis, sip Pimm's, sun yourself by the pool, or frolic with your dog through the club's rolling green hills. If you want to play croquet, you must wear white.

Many Englishmen (and even some Americans) have reciprocal memberships through their universities, so despite The Hurlingham's reputation as the most exclusive private members' club in England, it's not as hard to get into as people think.

My favorite event? Guy Fawkes Night (November 5). There is nothing better than a grand fireworks display, hot British boys, and hot mulled wine.

Polo in the Park and the Boat Race Ball are also worth attending, as is The Hurlingham's exclusive speed dating evening.

# Parable #4

I once found myself attending a black-tie ball for a charity that provides cricket equipment to disadvantaged children. (In England it doesn't matter if the child is starving or homeless, as long as he or she can play cricket.) I was seated at a table of rowdy rugby players and had already consumed several glasses of champagne before the first course arrived. It was salmon of some kind, yet I was so caught up in the ridiculous conversations happening around me (and so hungry, as I hadn't had much for lunch) that I accidentally used the wrong knife. I quickly spotted my mistake after the first bite and swiftly changed knives, certain no one would notice—least of all the highly inebriated gentlemen on either side of me.

How wrong I was.

Within seconds, the broad-shouldered, floppy-haired English-man to my right was standing up and tapping his spoon on his water glass to get the table's attention.

"I would like to announce that the lovely American to my left has used the wrong knife," Tarquin bellowed good-naturedly. "And for this she must be penalized!"

To atone for my mistake I was forced to chug the rest of my wine, the rest of Tarquin's wine, and all the remaining wine in the bottle sitting in the center of our table.

As you can imagine, I have very little recollection of what happened after that. But let me tell you: I now make a point of paying close attention to the cutlery before each and every course.

And so should you.

# Regal Hunting Ground #5: Formal Balls

At the turn of the century, a girl was never to be seen dancing twice with the same partner, and ladies *always* wore gloves on the dance floor because "flesh must never touch flesh." These days, British balls are slightly more relaxed. They may sound like remnants from Tudor times or the age of Cinderella, but black- or white-tie balls are actually extremely popular with London's young, professional set.

Over the years I've come to notice that the more formal the social event, the faster it spirals out of control. London balls actually remind me of American college formals—when, despite the glamorous dress codes, boys and girls still ended up sprawled drunkenly on the dance floor (or under the table). The fact that everyone at London balls are several years out of college doesn't seem to change the caliber of behavior. If anything, it's worse. (And I mean that in the best possible way.)

**What to expect:** Despite the philanthropic motivations, black-tie balls can be some of the most flirty and debaucherous affairs you will find anywhere in the UK. They usually take place in well-known London hotels and include a champagne reception followed by a seated three-course dinner and a few hours of dancing. Occasions to really dress up become less and less frequent with every generation, so when the opportunity presents itself—take it!

**Where to go:** Gather some friends and join a table at any of the following:

*The Royal Caledonian Ball* (affectionately known as "the Cally"), www.royalcaledonianball.com

The Royal Caledonian Ball began as a private gathering hosted by the Duke and Duchess of Atholl for all their Scottish friends who lived in London. By 1849, still at their invitation, the dance was held to raise funds for various Scottish charities. Records show that the ball has been held annually ever since (the only exceptions being during the Boer War, directly after the death of Edward VII, and during the First and Second World Wars). The Royal Caledonian has grown into one of the highlights of the London Season and is one of the oldest charity balls in the world.

**When and where:** Now held every May at the Grosvenor House on Park Lane (one of the largest ballrooms in London).

**Who goes:** Since the days of King Edward VII, the ball has

been honored with the patronage of the reigning monarch and can currently celebrate more than fifty years of patronage by HM Queen Elizabeth II.

**What to wear:** The dress code is white tie. Think floor-length skirts, bare arms, and diamonds. Tiaras are optional (and only if they're real). When taking part in the Scottish Reels, ladies who are of Scottish descent should wear appropriate clan sashes. There are strict rules about this and people take it very seriously, so make sure you know what you're doing.

*Queen Charlotte's Ball,* **www.londonseason.net**
An important fixture of the original Season (see Chapter 6), this ball was initially held at London's Grosvenor House. Recently re-

vived, it is now held alternately at Kensington Palace, the Dorchester Hotel, the Wallace Collection, the Treasury House, or the Savoy Hotel. The ball continues its long tradition of raising money to improve the health of mothers and babies; the West London hospital that used to benefit is now known as Queen Charlotte's Hospital.

**What to wear:** The event requires wearing a long white dress and curtseying beside a giant white cake. (Origins of which belong to the wife of King George III, who asked her favorite ladies-in-waiting to present her with a massive birthday cake.)

But don't let the virginal dress code and crazy cake custom deter you—Queen Charlotte's Ball is still a splendid place to see and be seen.

### *Hunt Balls Throughout the Country* (see also **Parable #1, p. 33** )

Foxhunting in the UK is nothing like any kind of hunting you will find in the US No one wears camouflage and Day-Glo orange, no one camps or eats cans of baked beans, and (this is the most important part) no one is officially allowed to kill anything— as hunting with dogs has been outlawed in England and Wales since 2004. So more than anything, joining a hunt is just an opportunity to wear great clothes, chat to floppy-haired Englishmen (aka hotties on horseback), watch the hounds, and see the countryside. You don't have to ride like Zara Phillips to go hunting or to be an ardent hunt follower—as long as you can hang on and aren't completely terrified of horses, you'll be fine. And if you don't own a horse, you can easily rent one for the day.

**When:** Late October to the end of March.

**What to wear:** Fabulous wool jacket (in black, blue, or tweed), cream jodhpurs, leather boots, a collarless shirt, leather gloves, riding hat.

**Where to find your nearest hunt:** Baily's Hunting Directory, www.bailyshuntingdirectory.com.

**Faux pas:** Mentioning the hunting ban (many are still very bitter about this); calling them "dogs" (they're "hounds").

For more information on correct hunting conduct, subscribe to *Horse and Hound Magazine*, www.horseandhound.co.uk.

You don't necessarily have to hunt at all in order to attend a hunt ball. Sometimes you merely have to own a ball gown and buy a ticket. Hunt balls generally take place in marquees attached to some elegant country house, and they are usually a delightful social mix of old English gentry, Bright Young Things, and inebriated students from the Royal Agricultural College. Dress code can be black- or white-tie, so make sure to double-check. Here is a short list of the most riveting (and most raucous) hunt balls in the country:

1. Beaufort, www.beauforthunt.com

2. Berkshire, www.berkshire-hunt.co.uk

3. Berwickshire, www.berwickshire-hunt.co.uk

4. Heythrop, www.heythrophunt.com

5. Ledbury, www.ledburyhunt.co.uk

6. Quorn, www.quorn-hunt.co.uk

7. Warwickshire, www.warwickshirehunt.co.uk

### The Young Lord's Taverners Ball
**www.lordstaverners.org**
This black-tie London gala is especially boisterous and popular among well-heeled twenty-somethings (not to mention the bittersweet setting of Parable #4, p. 151).

### Any Fundraising Ball Where Prince William or Prince Harry Is a Patron of the Charity
Prince William's favorite charities are listed below. (See "Harry Hunting," page 124, for a list of Harry's charities.)

## PRINCE WILLIAM'S CHARITIES:

*Centrepoint.* Provides emergency accommodation, support, information, and training for homeless young people in London. Prince William is a patron. (His mother was also a patron at the time of her death.) William is heavily involved in the charity and recently spent a night sleeping on the streets of London to help raise awareness. www.centrepoint.org.uk

*The Child Bereavement Charity.* Provides specialized support, information, and training to all those affected when a child or parent dies. Prince William, who knows all too well what it's like to lose a mother, is a patron and often holds private meetings with bereaved families and children supported by the charity. www.childbereavement.org.uk

*Tusk Trust.* Funds environmental conservation across Africa, combining the interests of people and wildlife alike. Prince William is a patron. www.tusk.org

*Raleigh International.* A UK-based educational development charity that aims to help people of all backgrounds and nationalities discover their full potential. Both Prince William and Kate Middleton are Raleigh alumni—Prince William went to Chile with Raleigh International in 2000, and Kate did the same in 2001. www.raleighinternational.org

*Absolute Return for Kids (ARK).* Delivers programs in the areas of health, education, and child protection across the globe. The Duke and Duchess of Cambridge made their first philanthropic appearance as a married couple at an ARK fundraiser in June 2011. www.arkonline.org

*Help for Heroes.* A charity formed to help those who have been wounded in Britain's current conflicts. Prince William gave a speech to launch the opening of a new rehabilitation center and frequently visits many of the wounded soldiers. www.helpforheroes.org.uk

*Royal Marsden Hospital.* A world-renown cancer center specializing in diagnosis, treatment, care, education, and research. William is president (a position previously held by his mother, Diana, Princess of Wales). www.royalmarsden.nhs.uk/home

*The Royal Society.* A fellowship of the world's most eminent scientists, the oldest scientific academy in continuous existence. http://royalsociety.org

*Henry van Straubenzee Memorial Fund.* Aims to lift Ugandan children out of poverty through education. Princes William and Harry are joint patrons. www.henryvanstraubenzeemf.org.uk

*SkillForce.* An education charity working with young people throughout Great Britain who are in danger of leaving school without the skills and qualifications they need to succeed in life. The Duke of Cambridge (an official patron) launched the SkillForce Prince's Award in recognition of the contribution that young people make to their communities. www.skillforce.org

*The Prince's Rainforests Project.* Founded by William's father, the Prince of Wales, to discourage deforestation rates and show the vital link between rain forests and climate change. Princes William and Harry appeared alongside their father and an animated frog in a recent public awareness film on the subject. www.rainforestsos.org

*Diana, Princess of Wales Memorial Fund.* Established in September 1997 to continue William's mother's humanitarian work throughout the world. www.theworkcontinues.org

*The American Friends of the Foundation of Prince William and Prince Harry.* Supports the UK Foundation of Prince William and Prince Harry and other charities that support at-risk youth, environmental conservation, and injured Armed Forces personnel. In July 2011, during his North American tour, Prince William played in his first ever American polo match at the Santa

Barbara Polo & Racquet Club to raise funds for this charity. www.foundationpolochallenge.com/foundation.html

*Fields in Trust.* Aims to ensure that everyone has access to outdoor space for sports, play, and recreation. Prince William is the patron of this charity's Queen Elizabeth II Fields Challenge, which creates playing fields throughout the UK in honor of the Queen's Diamond Jubilee. www.fieldsintrust.org

For more information on Prince William's philanthropic engagements, write to: The Foundation of Prince William and Prince Harry, St. James's Palace, London, SW1A 1BS, United Kingdom.

## How to Tie a Bow-Tie

A good-looking Englishman suddenly turns into a drop-dead gorgeous Englishman the second he dons a tuxedo (aka "dinner jacket"). If he has tied his own bow tie rather than used a tacky clip-on, even better. All girls should know how to properly tie a man's bow tie before a formal event. It's a relatively small skill, but if done correctly and with nonchalance it leaves a lasting impression (not to mention that Englishmen find women deftly tying things around their necks to be extremely sexy).

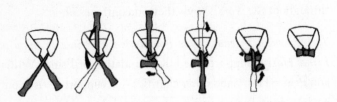

# Regal Hunting Ground # 6:
# Sailing and Skiing "Holidays"

Everyone seems so surprised to hear that until the Duke and Duchess of Cambridge embarked on their North American tour in June 2011, Kate Middleton had never traveled to the United States.* It's actually not that surprising. Young Brits in that elite social sphere don't really consider America to be a vacation destination. When the Castle Crew go on holiday, there are really only three options: safari holidays, sailing holidays, and skiing holidays. I'm not going to ask you to head to Africa just yet (after all, you only just landed in Great Britain), so in this section I will focus on the latter: sailing and skiing.

## Sailing

Most of the Castle Crew will have a father, grandfather, or boss who owns a boat—so if you want to seduce a Sloaney sailor, Cornwall or the Caribbean are your best bets. And while you may be picturing dazzling sunsets and countless cocktails on deck, the reality of most sailing holidays is an expectation to roll up your sleeves and actually help sail the boat—so you may want to brace yourself for abrupt orders and strange nautical jargon. (See "Sailing Lingo," page 164.) Please keep in mind that the boat must have real

---

* Prince William had been to America once before (in 2004), when he took a break from St. Andrews to visit an American friend, a Nashville heiress by the name of Anna Sloan, who was then studying at the University of Edinburgh. Anna had invited a group of their mutual friends to stay at her estate in Tennessee.

sails; if you're on a giant powerboat (or floating "gin palace") you're probably hanging out with the wrong crowd.

For steel drums and balmy sunshine, head to Mustique—a privately owned Caribbean island nestled in the Grenadine Islands of St.Vincent. Mustique is owned by Lord Glenconner, who purchased it more than fifty years ago. (He figured spending winters there with his family would be cheaper than heating his giant castle in the UK!) Lord Glenconner's island appeals to those who seek privacy and luxury, and in an age when we seem to know absolutely everything about royals and celebrities, Mustique is a place where they can be themselves. The island's carefree atmosphere has already nurtured two royal romances: Princess Margaret (the Queen's sister) and Lord Snowdon were regulars; and Prince William and Kate spent a romantic holiday here before their engagement.

As well as relaxing in a luxury villa, you can play Frisbee or volleyball on the beach, play tennis, or cruise around in a catamaran. If you and the Castle Crew are thirsty, head to Basil's Bar. (Prince William's favorite island drink is vodka and cranberry juice; Kate prefers piña coladas.)

*Also try:* Antigua (especially Antigua Race Week), The British Virgin Islands, The Greek Isles, and Croatia. (Harry was recently spotted dancing the night away in the latter.)

Cornwall is not as warm, but it's certainly easier (and much more affordable) to get to! In Cornwall, the Castle Crew are most likely to be found at the Mariners Rock pub, in the Cornish village of Rock. This seaside pub was thrust into the spotlight by Prince William and Prince Harry when they began visiting every year in the late nineties. It wasn't long before the princes were followed by hordes of British public boys from the likes of Eton, Marlborough, and Radley. (All good news for girls on the hunt!)

Rent a cottage for the weekend or stay in a quaint bed-and-breakfast. The drive is long (five hours from London by car or train), but it's worth the trip. The beachside hotspot is filled with cut-glass accents, blond highlights, Ray-Bans, and high-fashion flip-flops. But in addition to well-spoken Englishmen, there is plenty of sailing, surfing, and water-skiing to be had right down the road. Cornwall is known for delectable scones with clotted cream, and you won't find fresher fish and chips anywhere else. Again, the regal drink of choice is lashings of vodka and cranberry juice.

*Also try*: the Oyster Catcher in Polzeath and Falmouth Week in Cornwall.

Be warned: Brits flock to the Cornish coast at all times of year, regardless of the weather—it is not uncommon to see entire families wearing scarves and winter coats attempting to build sand castles on a wet and rainy beach.

(See also "Cowes Week," page 185.)

BOATING CHIC:

- Minimal makeup

- Flattering swimwear (or "swimming costume")

- Polo shirt from Crew Clothing, T&G, or Henry Lloyd

- Warm top to block out the wind

- Sporty waterproof jacket

- Sailing gloves

- Sunglasses

- Deck shoes from Sebago or Dubarry (heels and/or black soles have no place onboard)

## SAILING LINGO

Whenever I go sailing with my English husband, I usually have no idea what he's talking about.

"Ease the port side jib sheet," he'll tell me. I'll look around me utterly confused. All I have with me are my sunglasses. There are no sheets or blankets onboard.

Then he'll sigh with exasperation and say, "Please can you loosen the red-and-white rope on your left side that's wrapped around that metal thing?"

Why didn't he say so in the first place? That's the thing about boys who sail. They speak in code.

Apparently it's possible to jibe a jib but not jib a jibe, and a boat is never an *it* but a *she*–and that's only the beginning of this crazy language. So whether you're a sailing novice like me (and in my defense, I grew up in a landlocked state) or a nautical expert, it's good to know some of the sailing lingo. Here is a cheat sheet for you to study next time you're off to Cornwall, the Caribbean, or Cowes.

SAILING CHEAT SHEET:

- **port:** the left-hand side of the boat ("There's no port left in the bottle" helps me to remember.)

- **starboard:** the right-hand side of the boat

- **bow:** the front of the boat (the pointy end)

- **stern:** the back of the boat

- **boom:** the horizontal pole that holds the mainsail and moves from side to side (Getting in its way can be dangerous—I've even heard horror stories of beheadings—so when in doubt, stay low.)

- **knot:** a nautical mile per hour (roughly equivalent to 1.15 miles per hour )

- **skipper:** the boat's helmsman or captain (*not* Barbie's younger sister)

- **sheet:** a rope (that looks nothing like a sheet) attached to the sail or boom

- **painter:** a rope (that has nothing to do with painting) attached to the front of a small boat

- **jib:** a triangular sail stretching from the masthead to the boom

- **jibe:** to shift a sail from one side to the other going downwind

- **tack:** to shift a sail from one side to the other going upwind

- **berth:** a place occupied by a boat in a harbor; also how many people can sleep on the boat (e.g., "the yacht has eight berths" means she can sleep eight people)

- **galley:** kitchen on a boat

- **head:** toilet ("loo"!) on a boat

- **buoy:** an anchored flotation ball used to mark a position in the water

- **capsize:** when the boat turns over ninety degrees and everyone falls out

## Avoiding Sea Sickness

It can happen to even the most experienced sailing girls, so here are some tips for negating any bouts of nautical nausea.

- Avoid going below deck any longer than you have to.

- Do not attempt to read books, magazines, maps, emails, or text messages while onboard.

- Fresh air definitely helps, so keep the wind in your face and take deep breaths.

- Focus your attention on a fixed point on the horizon.

- Ask if you can help steer the boat (also a good way to flirt with the skipper).

- Drink plenty of water—dehydration can make you feel dizzy.

- Eat light meals and avoid getting hungry—hunger pains can make you feel dizzy.

- Take a motion sickness pill (like Dramamine) *before* you get sick (they are not effective if taken afterward).

# Skiing

You definitely don't want to go after any English guy who spends less than a week a year in the Alps.

If you're a good skier, you'll easily be able to impress him with your US-honed powder skills (the snow on American slopes is much better than in Europe, where they are accustomed to skiing on virtual ice). But if you're a terrible skier it doesn't really matter—in the Alps, the emphasis is more about eating and drinking (mainly drinking) in the fresh mountain air than it is about actual skiing. It's about renting a big mountain cabin (called a "chalet") with a group of friends, having breakfast and dinner cooked for you every day by a pretty "chalet girl," and drinking yourself into oblivion.

Whereas American resorts wouldn't dream of putting nightclubs on their ski slopes and inviting the lawsuits that are sure to result by allowing skiers to do shots of Jägermeister before their black diamond runs, Europe is much more laid back about such things. If you want to ride the last lift to the top of the mountain, drink yourself silly at a slope-side bar, then ski back down in the pitch-black night with nothing but a handheld fire torch to guide you (this actually happens)—go for it!

Après skiing festivities ("after" skiing festivities) are a big deal, and there is a princely party going on somewhere every single night. So grab a group of girls and book your chalet at any of the following:

### Klosters (Switzerland)

**Who goes:** The King and Queen of Sweden, Prince Andrew, Prince Harry, and the Duke and Duchess of Cambridge. (In 2004, Klosters was the setting of Kate and Will's first public kiss.) Klosters is also famous for being the favorite resort of Prince Charles.

**Where to stay:** The Walserhof hotel, which boasts a Michelin-starred restaurant. www.walserhof.ch

### Verbier (Switzerland)

Verbier is *the* place to be for the young jet set. When William and Harry go on family vacations, they go to Klosters, but when they go to party with friends, they go to Verbier.

**Who goes there:** Prince Harry, William and Kate, The Duchess of York, Hugh Grant, James Blunt, and Jamie Oliver. Princess Eugenie met her boyfriend Jack Brooksbank here when she was celebrating her father, Prince Andrew's fiftieth birthday.

**Best après ski:** The Farm Club (a Sloane Ranger mecca!), the Coco Club, and PUBLIC Verbier. (Club owner Guy Pelly noticed that the same folks that love PUBLIC London are the same folks that head to the slopes of Verbier in the winter. So he figured why not bring their favorite London club directly to the Alps?) www .public.uk.com

**What to drink at the Coco Club (only if someone else is buying):** The Ice Chalet—a concoction of champagne and cognac, served in a hand-carved chalet ice sculpture with straws sticking through the roof. The good news is it serves eight people; the bad news is it costs $7,300. For those who want something cheaper, there is the $960 Avalanche cocktail that comes in a mountain-shaped glass dotted with Swarovski crystals.

### Val d'Isere (France)

There are so many Sloane Rangers in this elite French resort, Val d'Isere has been dubbed "Val Sloane Square."

**Best après ski:** Dick's Tea Bar, www.dicksteabar.com

### Lech (Austria)

Perfect for discreet old-money types.

**Who goes there:** Queen Beatrix and the Dutch royal family. This was also a beloved favorite of the late Princess Diana.

**Where to stay:** Hotel Arberg, www.arlberghotel.at

*Zermatt (Switzerland)*

**Who goes there:** William and Kate, the Duchess of York, Princesses Beatrice, Princess Eugenie, Madonna.

**Best après ski:** Heimberg Bar, the Brown Cow Pub.

*Meribel (France)*

**Who goes there:** Prince Felipe of Spain, the Earl and Countess of Wessex.

**Where to stay:** If you want to mix with royalty and the aristocracy, book your chalet with Scott Dunn, www.scottdunn.com/luxury-holiday/ski-holidays.

# More Regal Hunting Grounds

## The Oxford vs. Cambridge Boat Race

River Thames, London, www.theboatrace.org

A tradition since 1829, this 4.25-mile rowing race between England's most prestigious and illustrious universities is one of the flirtiest afternoons in the London social calendar. I love it because the race itself is exciting, and even better, it's over in less than twenty minutes. After that, the day is all about socializing with cute (ever so tipsy) British boys along the sunny riverbank.

**Who are the rowers:** All handsome, all insanely intelligent, all insanely tall. (Most are six-foot-five or taller.) Remember the scarily attractive Winklevoss twins in the movie *The Social Network*? They rowed in this race a few years ago.

**Where to go:** Anywhere on the towpath between Putney Bridge and Hammersmith (get there early to ensure a good viewing spot).

The Crabtree Pub is also a good base. Afterward, crash a party at any of the nearby rowing clubs.

## Scottish Dancing Events (aka "Reels")

Not nearly as nerdy as it sounds. This weekly hobby is extremely trendy and increasingly popular among well-heeled London single-tons. A brilliant way to learn something new and dance with gorgeous British boys.

**What to expect:** Scottish-style square dancing (but you don't need to know the steps to attend a session, as the MC will talk you through it all, dance by dance).

**What to wear:** The practice sessions are casual, but the formal balls will require an actual ball gown.

**Bonus:** Many reels take place at The Hurlingham Club www.royalcaledonianball.com/other_events.

RECOMMENDED READING:

*Gone with the Windsors* by Laurie Graham

This is one of my favorite novels of all time. It's the fictional diary of Wallis Simpson's best American friend, Maybell, and her hilarious descriptions of American girls crashing the upper-class parties of 1930s Britain. Lots of yachts, lots of dresses, lots of diamonds. And if you can't stomach nonfiction, *Gone with the Windsors* is a lighthearted way to get the scoop on the clever divorcée from Baltimore who stole the heart of a king. I promise you will laugh out loud.

*The American Heiress* **by Daisy Goodwin**

For those of you who love Lady Cora, the (American) Countess of Grantham in *Downton Abbey*, this sparkling novel is based on a very similar American character, who just happens to go by the very same name. It tells the tale of a bright-eyed American girl named Cora Cash, who travels to England, determined to find the one thing money can't buy in the US—a title. Of course Cora must navigate the murky waters of Old World aristocrats and obscure codes of conduct (something all American girls in contemporary London will relate to).

# SIX

# THE SEASON

*The American invasion has done English society
a great deal of good. American women are bright,
clever, and wonderfully cosmopolitan . . . In the art
of amusing men they are adept, both by nature and
education, and can actually tell a story without
forgetting the point—an accomplishment that is
extremely rare among the women of other countries.*
—OSCAR WILDE

To be honest, I had never been one for spectator sports. Back in America, I would have rather done just about anything than watch baseball or football or almost any other game involving a ball. I just couldn't focus on any of it. Sometimes I felt like I might as well be watching fish swim back and forth in a tank.

But then I discovered the British *Season*.

Sure there are sports involved but it's so much more elegant, so much more civilized, and usually there's champagne being handed to me at some point. (In fact, it's quite easy for all of the Season events to simply blur into one long, alcoholic picnic.) So from a girl who at one time would've rather died than gone to another sporting event, I've been entirely converted. And so will you.

# A Brief History

Prior to 1958, well-bred English girls (aka "debutantes") were formally presented to the Queen to symbolically mark their debut into aristocratic society. This was followed by a nonstop string of social events known as "the Season." In the beginning, the Season was defined by the movements of the royal family, who only lived in London between May and August. During these months, the aristocracy would also reside in the capital and this very social time of year became integral to the aristocratic marriage market.

This is how it worked: At the tender age of seventeen, upper-class English girls were launched into society with a formal curtsey to the monarch—also known as being presented "at Court."

Girls had to be presented to the Queen by a female relative who had also been presented to the Queen when she was seventeen (otherwise they were not allowed to take part in the Season).

After the big curtsey, the parents of each debutante hosted a black-tie ball at which their daughter would officially "debut." These balls were interspersed with a whirlwind of cocktail parties and lots of fun summer sporting events. Most "debs" went out at least five nights a week, usually costing their families up to $200,000 in today's money. (That's a lot of dresses.)

The ultimate purpose of all these parties was to display the young, aristocratic girls to the young, aristocratic boys. The lucky bachelors were usually the sons of UK nobility and gentry, and known to everyone as "the debs' delights." Needless to say, it was every debutante's goal to be engaged to one of them by the end of the Season.

The debutantes were really the first "It Girls" and celebrity fashion plates of their kind, and as you can imagine, the society photographers loved them. Still, deb etiquette was rigorous. A young woman could flirt and go on dates, but virginity was a must. Young men who tried to go too far were blacklisted as NSIT (Not Safe in Taxis).*

Believe me, if I could be born into another era, this would be the one I would choose! Life was one big Nancy Mitford† novel! Sadly, I was born in Colorado in the late twentieth century, and by the time I made it to London, the traditional nineteenth-century English Season had morphed into something else entirely. After World War II, English society became slightly more egalitarian, and the strict social constraints of the original Season could no longer survive. Blue-blooded families were slowly being overtaken by new money, and some sly aristocratic mothers began charging a fee to present unconnected nouveau riche girls to the Queen.

As Princess Margaret infamously declared, "We had to put a stop to it. Every tart in London was getting in." And so in 1958, Queen Elizabeth ended the antiquated practice of Court presentations altogether. Luckily, there are still some surviving remnants of the original Season for those in the know to enjoy . . .

---

* To be fair, NSIT applies to every British boy I've ever met.

† You know what I'm going to say: If you haven't already, start reading Nancy Mitford asap. Start with *The Pursuit of Love* and *Love in a Cold Climate*.

**THREE THINGS TO REMEMBER ABOUT THE SEASON:**

1. When attending any of the following events, it's important *not* to go through a heavily logo-ed form of corporate entertaining. If a corporate invite is your only option, then don't turn it down, but please keep in mind that you won't be experiencing the real deal.

2. Although all of these events occur between the months of May and August (which is technically referred to as "summer"), please note that you are in the United Kingdom and sunshine is a privilege not an assumption. Despite the strict summery dress codes required by many of these venues, be prepared for cold and/or wet weather *at all times*. This means smiling through the shivering drizzle and being a good sport about wearing wellies with your best sundress. Learning to enjoy yourself in freezing weather is terribly English, so you might as well get used to it.

3. Several of these events require setting up a formal picnic in a grassy parking lot (remnants of an era when everyone had servants to unpack the hamper and lay the best china out for a quick luncheon). Hence, you must perfect the art of wearing a crisp linen suit (with matching hat), sitting in a lawn chair in the middle of a crowded parking lot (quite often in the rain), and eating soggy salmon sandwiches off your lap while sipping champagne, making witty repartee, and looking like you're having the time your life. Master this with grace and aplomb, and you have mastered the British Season.

Audrey Hepburn at Royal Ascot in *My Fair Lady*.

*Every duke and earl and peer is here*
*Everyone who should be here is here.*
*What a smashing, positively dashing*
*Spectacle: at the Ascot opening day.*
—FROM THE FILM *MY FAIR LADY*

## Royal Ascot
Berkshire, www.ascot.co.uk

**When:** Four days every year in June.

**What to expect:** Thoroughbred racehorses, gentlemen in top hats, It Girls in Philip Treacy, an air of glamour and exclusivity.

**Who goes:** Each day at Royal Ascot, the Queen and her party drive in open-topped carriages across Windsor Park, entering the racecourse through the Golden Gates.

**Where to go:**

- *The Royal Enclosure.* Originally established in the 1790s to ensure privacy for members of the royal family, this exclusive area was once only accessible to guests brandishing a royal invitation. The Royal Enclosure allows access to the best viewing areas and facilities on the course, as well as use of the Enclosure Gardens. These days, you can write to the US Embassy and ask politely for an invite, be invited by someone who has attended previously, or make a reservation for lunch at one of the restaurants inside. Be warned that convicted criminals and bankrupts are banned from the Royal Enclosure; divorcées have only been allowed since 1955.

- *Parties and Picnics in Car Park #1.* Bizarrely, these are a very big deal. Some members of British society never even bother to leave this particular Ascot parking lot, assuming that royals and races couldn't possibly compete with their own exclusive festivities.

**What to wear:\*** Only a formal day dress or suit (knee-length or longer) paired with a proper hat is acceptable. (A headpiece that has a base of four inches or more in diameter is also satisfactory.) Keep in mind that it's easy to go overboard with look-at-me outfits and crazy headgear, but try to strike a balance between conservative and fashionable. Gentlemen are required to wear either black

---

\* The dress code differs between Royal Ascot and all other Ascot race days, so please ensure you are dressed appropriately for the enclosure on the race day you have booked.

or gray morning dress, which must include a waistcoat, tie (not a cravat), black or gray top hat, and black shoes. (Rod Stewart was once infamously turned away for wearing trendy sneakers with his morning suit.) A gentleman may only remove his top hat within a restaurant, private box, or private club, or within that facility's terrace, balcony, or garden.

**What NOT to wear:** Miniskirts, strapless dresses, halter neck dresses, spaghetti strap dresses, dresses with a strap less than one inch wide, anything that exposes the midriff, anything that is sheer or has sheer straps. (Jackets and pashminas are allowed, but the dresses and tops underneath must still comply with the Royal Enclosure dress code.)

**What to bring:** Binoculars.

**Top tips:** Don't bother with the odds, the bookies, or the stats in the *Racing Post*. Just have a look at the "starters" in the paddock, then bet a few pounds on the handsomest horse with the cutest name. Make sure you have a good spot at the finish line to watch your horse thunder past and to cheer him into the winners enclosure (although please don't emulate Eliza Doolittle as you do this).

**Inside info:** The jockey wearing the black silk cap and purple silk jacket with red sleeves and gold braiding is riding for the Queen.

**Best flirting spot:** Amid the young, hip, and fashionable at the Birdcage pop-up party tent (within the Royal Enclosure Gardens)—a gilded shelter for the golden youth. www.royalascot birdcage.com

**Also try:** The Epsom Derby.

In 2008, racecourse owners at Ascot were forced to issue dress code guidance, which suggested women "wear knickers, but not on show." Surely that's sound advice for *any* social event—royal or otherwise—but maybe that's just me. In 2012 (and not a moment too soon), the dress code at Ascot was completely revised to restore decorum to the age-old event, and organizers promise that it will be rigorously enforced. Let's hope so. After all, Ascot is, in the words of one race official, a formal occasion—"not one where you dress as you would at a nightclub."

Indeed. Which brings me to . . .

**What to avoid at Ascot:** Anything outside the safe confines of the Royal Enclosure. Despite the nearby presence of the Queen of England herself, nothing stops dozens of pink stretch limos from various London lap dancing clubs from pulling into the grandstand next door. On this side of the fence you will see hundreds of drunk, tattooed race-goers blatantly ignoring the dress code (there is more flesh on display in the Silver Ring of Ascot than during spring break at Daytona Beach), throwing up on each other and starting fistfights. I wish I were exaggerating about this, but I'm not. I see blood spilled every single year. Extremely upsetting; not to mention disrespectful to such a historic royal tradition.

Luckily, from 2012 onward, women in the less formal Grandstand will be required to wear a hat or fascinator and to cover both their shoulders and their midriffs. Shorts are also no longer permitted. (Hallelujah.) However, the *even less formal* Silver Ring still has no formal dress code whatsoever. But thanks to the new rules, at least bare chests are no longer permissible, and fancy dress, novelty, and promotional clothing are not allowed on-site. I'm all for this. But personally, I'll believe it when I see it.

# The Henley Royal Regatta
Henley-on-Thames, Oxfordshire, www.hrr.co.uk

**When:** This world-renowned rowing event is held over five days (Wednesday to Sunday) in late June or early July. This event is very male, very private school, and very, very English. (Not surprisingly, it's one of my favorites.)

**Where to go:** The general public can enjoy races from various points along the Thames towpath, but the Stewards' Enclosure, at the end of the course, is where you need to be. This is where the final awards ceremony takes place, but access is limited to Stewards (former rowers who organize the regatta), members of the Enclosure, and their guests.

**What to expect:** Rolling green lawns, covered grandstands, riverside restaurants and bars.

**Who goes:** Strapping Englishmen who once rowed for Oxford or Cambridge wearing silly wool blazers in the blazing sun. Prince Albert became the royal patron of Henley in 1851, and since this date the reigning monarch has stood as official patron to the event.

**What to wear:** Summery dresses below the knee. (The dress code in the Stewards' Enclosure is notoriously strict. One of my friends was forced to pull her skirt below her bottom and cover her exposed derriere with a long cardigan in order to pass through the gates.) Bare shoulders are fine. Hats are not required. High heels will sink into the grassy banks, so best if you opt for cute wedges.

**What to drink:** Pimm's and lemonade.

**Best flirting spot:** By day? The Leander Club. By night? The Mahiki Tent (the latter requires tickets, so book in advance, www.mahiki.com).

**Faux pas:** Pantsuits, cell phones.

HELPFUL ROWING JARGON:

- **coxswain (aka "Cox"):** the person facing the back of the boat responsible for steering and race strategy (normally the one doing all the shouting)

- **sculler:** a rower who rows with two oars, one in each hand

- **stroke:** the rower closest to the back of the boat, responsible for the stroke rate and rhythm

- **stroke rate:** the number of strokes executed per minute by a crew

PLANNING THE PERFECT "CAR PARK" PICNIC

- Whether you're packing a picnic for Royal Ascot or the Henley Royal Regatta, concentrate on elegant finger food that can be nibbled with minimal mess—the less cutlery required the better.

- Create an al fresco picnic menu that incorporates Britain's classic summer delicacies—things like asparagus, smoked salmon, and fresh strawberries. Always ensure that white wine, rosé, champagne, and beer are served chilled.

- It sounds crazy, but tables and chairs are a must for such picnics. Try to find ones that will easily collapse in the back of your car or taxi.

- Special touches make all the difference, and British guests *will notice* if you're not using starched table linens, proper wineglasses, and real champagne flutes.

&#10086; Ideally, food is packed in an old-fashioned willow picnic basket with leather trim, from Fortnum and Mason. (Even better, get them to cater the whole thing for you.) www .fortnumandmason.com

# Pimm's

The English summer is not complete without pitchers and pitchers of Pimm's. The British serve it at garden parties, at picnics, and during languid rounds of afternoon croquet; Pimm's lubricates all cricket matches and is the number one drink of choice at Wimbledon. (It is also safe to say that without Pimm's, Henley would be no more than a stilted formal gathering on a riverbank.)

Pimm's is a gin-based liquor that contains a top-secret mix of herbs that give it an amber-colored tint. Tasting subtly of citrus fruit and spices, Pimm's can be served both on ice or in cocktails. However, it is traditionally mixed with English "lemonade" (the kind that is clear and carbonated and vaguely similar to Sprite), along with a variety of chopped fruit, mint, and cucumber. The resulting concoction is not unlike a very large and very boozy cup of fruit cocktail. (Sometimes it's actually served with a long-handled spoon.)

Pimm's proffers a somewhat restrained 25 percent alcohol content, and its widespread popularity among the English summer events is undoubtedly based on the fact that it is light enough to be consumed all afternoon—while still being strong enough to provide the necessary party-time kick. If you hate alcoholic drinks that taste like alcoholic drinks, then you'll love Pimm's. Just try not to drink more than ten pints in a single afternoon.

### Classic Pimm's Recipe

1. Take a jug or tall glass and fill it with ice.
2. Mix 1 part Pimm's No. 1 with 3 parts sparkling lemonade (I prefer Schweppes's).
3. Add sliced cucumber, orange, lemon, and strawberries (I like to freeze these in advance so they act as extra ice cubes).
4. Garnish with a few sprigs of mint.

## Wimbledon
Wimbledon, London, www.wimbledon.org

**What is it:** The world's oldest major tennis championship and the only one still played on grass.

**When:** Two weeks between late June and early July.

**What to expect:** Strawberries and cream, pristine green lawns, and sexy tennis whites.

**What to drink:** Pimm's. What else?

**Who goes:** The Duke or Duchess of Kent usually presents the prizes to the winners of the Ladies' and Gentlemen's Singles and Doubles, and all players must bow or curtsey to the occupants of the Royal Box. Kate Middleton and her sister, Pippa, made a fashionable splash during their first public courtside appearance in 2011, and palace aides are reportedly discussing the idea of Kate taking over the trophy presenting duties in her new role as Duchess of Cambridge—which would surely add an exciting touch of glamour to the tournament. (Kate is an accomplished tennis player and used to play regularly at the Chelsea Harbor Club.*)

**Top tip:** Plan ahead and apply for tickets via the public online lottery system in *December*; otherwise be prepared to stand in line overnight for the same day's matches.

**Best flirting spot:** The Centre Court.


## Cowes Week
Isle of Wight, www.cowesweek.co.uk

Cowes Week is the longest-running yacht regatta in existence. The nautical event stages 40 daily races for more than 1,000 boats and up to 8,500 competitors participate each day. During Cowes Week, most sailing clubs open their doors to other UK yacht club members. You can also mix with the well-heeled West London crowd at the Mahiki or Raffles pop-up parties found along the neighboring marinas.

**When:** Eight days in early August.

**Who goes:** Both the Duke of Edinburgh and the Princess Royal have competed in Cowes as individuals.

**What to wear:** On the water? Gill or Musto. On the shore? Crew Clothing, T&G, Henry Lloyd. Shoes? Sebago or Dubarry.

**Best flirting spot:** During the fireworks grand finale on the final Friday of the regatta.

**Faux pas:** Seasickness, women in overly nautical-themed outfits.

**Also try:** Antigua Race Week, Falmouth Week.

(See also "Sailing," page 161.)

---

* FYI: This a great gym to join if you want to meet more of the Castle Crew; it was also the favored gym of the late Princess Diana. www.harbourclubchel sea.com

# Polo

Polo is the sexiest sport on the planet: gorgeous, strapping (often royal) players on horseback in hot pursuit of the ball, thundering hooves, bits of grass, clouds of dust, the loud smack of the mallet . . . the entire event is the epitome of sportsmanship, valor, and equestrian skill. After attending my very first polo match and applauding the game between sips of champagne, I understood completely why polo had been the royal sport of choice for so many centuries: "Let other people play at other things. The King of Games still remains the Game of Kings."*

TOP 5 POLO EVENTS:

1. The Prince of Wales Trophy at the Royal County of Berkshire, www.rcbpoloclub.com

2. The Queen's Cup at Guards (I love this one because Her Majesty is always in attendance), www.guardspoloclub.com

3. The Warwickshire Cup at Cirencester Park
   www.cirencesterpolo.co.uk

4. The Gold Cup at Cowdray Park, www.cowdraypolo.co.uk

5. Cartier International at Guards (the pinnacle of the polo calendar but increasingly less elite that the others)
   www.guardspoloclub.com

---

* A phrase carved beside an ancient polo ground in Southern Asia.

**The game:** Two teams of four, all on horseback, gallop around a lawn three times the size of a soccer field, attempting to hit a small white ball with long-handled mallets.

**When:** The polo season runs from April to September.

**Where to go:** You can typically choose between grandstand seating and eating a picnic on the lawn or more exclusive members' enclosures that offer a lavish sit-down lunch and continuous champagne. Lunch comes first, then the polo.

**What to drink:** Veuve Clicquot.

**What to wear:** Your entry badge, designer shades, a smart sundress, flats or wedges.

**Faux pas:** Stiletto heels, insanely short hemlines (as the saying goes, people are there to see the ponies' legs, not yours).

**Best flirting spots:** The Jack Wills Eton vs. Harrow match at Guards Polo Club (think of the cute alumni!), the Chinawhite party tent at Cartier International (Prince Harry and his chums frequently make an appearance).

POLO POINTERS:

- Call them polo *ponies*, NOT horses. A good polo pony can stop and turn on a dime (or a sixpence!), and most players would say that their success is primarily due to their ponies' skill. (FYI: Ponies' legs are often bandaged for support and protection—not because they are injured.)

- A *chukka* is a period of play (similar to a tennis set), lasting seven minutes. At the end of each chukka, the ponies are swapped so they don't get too tired. A full game has eight chukkas; club matches have four to six.

🍬 *Divots* are the holes made on the field by all those pounding hooves. Spectators are encouraged to stomp them back down at halftime (another good reason to wear flats or wedges instead of heels).

# Parable #5

I know a pretty twenty-something girl from California (let's call her Clara) who loves England more than life itself. And I admire her more than I can say. She works hard at her job in America and saves up so she can come to England every year to do the Season. And do the Season she does! She has dresses specially made for the Royal Enclosure (the clothes in Los Angeles are too slutty, she tells me), and she even designs and sews her own hats (she is determined, among other things, to become a part-time milliner). She goes to *all* of Henley (not just one day) and *all* of Royal Ascot and to every single polo match that matters. At night you can find her in Boujis and Mahiki, and on her free afternoons she heads to Gloucestershire (where Prince Charles has a country estate) to hang out with the bright young Brits known as the "Glossy Posse." I'm telling you, if she doesn't at least *kiss* Prince Harry one day—I'll be very surprised.

Anyway, what I love about Clara is her pure tenacity. She knows the life she wants and she goes after it. To obtain entrance into the elite enclosures of English polo clubs, you must be a member, and to become a member you must be recommended by a member. Clara wasn't daunted. From her desk in LA, she wrote a letter to each membership secretary of each polo club she wanted to attend. She politely explained how much she loved polo and kindly asked that they grant her a special summer membership without the required recommendation. And you know what? Every single one of them agreed. Due to the strength of her all-American perseverance, Clara arrived in the UK with a handful of entry badges that most British polo fans would kill for.

The lesson? Nothing ventured; nothing gained.

## The Chelsea Flower Show
Royal Hospital, Chelsea, www.rhs.org.uk/chelsea

**When:** five days in May

**What is it:** This world-famous flower show is a traditional highlight of the British summer Season and is a particular favorite of the Royal Family. Founded in the mid-nineteenth century by the Royal Horticultural Society (RHS), the Chelsea Flower Show takes over the grounds of the Royal Hospital with a huge array of creative floral displays.

**What to expect:** Rubbing shoulders with royalty as you wander through exquisite exhibits of floristry.

**Who goes:** The Queen, Charles, and Camilla are almost always in attendance for the Royal Preview, which takes place on the Monday. (In 2002, Prince Charles was an actual exhibitor; his display was called the "Healing Garden" and featured a tribute to his late grandmother.) Prince Albert of Monaco has also been known to make an appearance—maybe one day he'll bring his hot nephews Andrea and Pierre.

**What to wear:** There is no stringent dress code, but ladies should wear a summery dress or skirt with a smart jacket or cardigan. Hats are not required, but you may want to plan for wet weather.

**Top tip:** Become a member of the Royal Horticultural Society. RHS members enjoy special rates and privileged entry. Advance booking is essential.

**Faux pas:** Holding a 9-to-5 job. (This event is designed purely for ladies who lunch and is not open on Saturday or Sunday.)

## Glorious Goodwood
Goodwood Park, West Sussex, www.goodwood.co.uk

**What is it:** King Edward VII famously described this prestigious horse racing event as a fabulous "garden party with racing tacked on." Not much has changed since.

**Where:** Goodwood was the ancestral home of the Duke of Richmond for more than three hundred years and boasts a superb collection of paintings, porcelain, and furniture.

**What to expect:** "Panamas, Pimm's, and parasols" along the rolling lawns of this spectacular stately home.

**What to wear:** For the Richmond Enclosure, men should don linen suits, waistcoats, and the archetypal Panama hat popularized by King Edward VII. Ladies should aim for understated glamour and chic elegance (think floaty dresses) and are encouraged to wear hats at the Festival Meeting.

**Also try:** The Goodwood Festival of Speed—the largest motor sports party in the world, popularly dubbed "the garden party of the Gods," and the Goodwood Revival—think fabulous vintage cars and fabulous vintage clothes.

## Glyndebourne
East Sussex, www.glyndebourne.com

**What is it:** This world-class opera festival presents yet another opportunity to enjoy a champagne picnic on a stately summer lawn. (When I said the season is one long alcoholic picnic, I wasn't kidding.) Dating back more than seventy years, Glyndebourne (which rhymes with "kind-born") attracts opera fans from all over the world to indulge in outdoor renditions of Mozart and Handel. Catered picnics, along with garden furniture and your own private butler, can easily be arranged.

**Dress code:** Black-tie (yes, you read that correctly—a black-tie picnic!). This means wear a short or long evening dress. The tradition of wearing evening dress during the Glyndebourne Festival originated with founder John Christie, who felt it helped the audience show respect for the performers. Given the perils of the British weather, it is also advisable to bring an additional, warm layer: cardigan, pashmina, raincoat, etc.

# The Summer Exhibition at the Royal Academy
Piccadilly, London, www.royalacademy.org.uk

**What to expect:** Beautiful people swanning around and chatting about art. (Perfect for putting that new History of Art degree of yours to good use.)

RECOMMENDED READING:

### *Last Curtsey* by Fiona MacCarthy
This is a glorious firsthand account of the 1958 English Season. The author was lucky enough to be in the last group of debutantes to actually go to Buckingham Palace and curtsey to the Queen. Fiona describes how she and her fellow teenage "debs" took part in some of the last rituals of aristocratic power and indulged in a British social season that had remained unchanged since the eighteenth century. The author tells of riotous party seasons that stretched on for months, flitting in and out of the grand houses of London, dancing and flirting with young noblemen everywhere

from the Home Counties to the Scottish Highlands. I wanted to *live* in this book's pages. So will you.

### *Snobs* by Julian Fellowes

This novel is the tale of Edith Lavery. Edith is a middle-class English girl who goes to Royal Ascot and bags one of the most eligible bachelors in the country—Charles Broughton, heir to the Marquess of Uckfield. Edith soon becomes a countess, yet life among the upper echelons of society is not all that it seems. She quickly discovers there is much more to the aristocracy than dancing at Annabel's and understanding which fork to use at dinner. And then there is Charles's mother, the frightening Lady Uckfield, who is none too pleased with her son's choice of wife. From the screenwriter that brought us *Gosford Park* and our beloved *Downton Abbey*, *Snobs* is the best, and funniest, contemporary British novel I've read in years.

SEVEN

# DATING

*Charles: Do you think there really are*
*people who can just go up and say, "Hi, babe.*
*Name's Charles. This is your lucky night."?*

*Matthew: Well, if there are, they're not English.*
—FROM THE FILM *FOUR WEDDINGS AND A FUNERAL*

Every time I go back to America, I'm always struck by how dif-ferent the single men are from their British counterparts. Yes, American men are louder and a bit more confident (bordering on cocky), but what really strikes me is they are not afraid to show their interest in you—any time, any place.

One afternoon, when I was visiting my cousin in New York, I was standing on the train platform at Penn Station, when a guy approached me and gave me his business card; one hour later while I was having lunch with my cousin in Union Square, another guy passed me his phone number on a cocktail napkin. It's all so cliché, but deep down I love that American men have the guts to do these things! (And even better, that they do these things when they are sober!)

British women would probably find this forward American behavior a little freaky, but I have a hunch that they might also find it slightly refreshing, because British men won't give you their business cards unless it's two in the morning and they've consumed at least ten pints' worth of Dutch courage. Despite their inebriated state, they'll manage to slur something surprisingly charming and eloquent (they are English after all), then they'll rugby tackle you into a dark corner, stick their tongue down your throat, and take you home. When you wake up in the morning, you are boyfriend and girlfriend. I can't tell you how many English couples have met this way.

After I graduated from college, my closest friends were scattered across the globe: LA, Chicago, DC, New York, London— the list of cities made it sound as if we were opening a chain of fashion boutiques. But in the UK, after graduation everyone moves to London. So most single English girls in their twenties are still hanging out with the same group of friends they had in college. Considering that in college they only became friends with "suitable" types anyway (boys and girls that went to appropriate boarding schools) and their families had been going to parties in each other's country houses for generations—getting drunkenly kissed in a pub by one of them several years later is hardly a big deal.

The two of them might be boyfriend and girlfriend for a year or two, and then she might move on and become the girlfriend of another guy from her same selective peer group—and basically, whichever guy from this social circle rugby tackles her around the age of twenty-nine is the one she marries.

Shakespeare and other medieval English poets may have invented courtly love, but I can safely say without reservation that the modern English male knows little or nothing about courtship.

## Beyond the Looking Glass

By the time I reached the age of eighteen, I had never actually encountered a living, breathing Englishman. I had never heard a living, breathing English accent that wasn't in a Hugh Grant movie, a BBC costume drama, or an old rerun of *Fawlty Towers*. So when I heard one for the first time (in the beer-stained basement of a noisy fraternity house), the effect was positively hypnotic.

I felt like someone raised by wolves who had suddenly recognized the sound of my mother tongue even if I couldn't speak it myself. I felt like the kid in *The Jungle Book* when he first saw another human. The sound of that upper-crust accent evoked my deepest memories and innermost desires, and in that beautiful, emotionally charged moment, I became some kind of English accent–addicted madwoman.

So as you can imagine, when I moved to the UK two years later, and Rupert introduced me to the Bright Young Things, I was beside myself. I was attracted to almost no one at my American college, and even less so at my hickville high school—and yet quite shockingly, I wanted to make out with every single male in arm's reach that spoke to me in a plummy English accent! And let me tell you: It scared the daylights out of me.

These beautiful boys with their beautiful accents seemed to be from an enchanted world. A world of family crests, family castles, boarding schools, and black-tie dinner parties. Their carefree conversations were more witty and intellectual than anything I'd ever heard, and they spoke to me with a James Bond–style charm that I found irresistible, about topics that I found utterly intriguing.

I think part of it was that I was so very different from them—and bridging that chasm of difference was an exhilarating aphrodisiac. Making actual physical contact with an idea that for years had seemed so out of reach was to me like making contact with a magical world beyond the looking glass. When it came to British men, my heart and mind were hooked. How could I turn back?

## Lie Back and Think of England

*I am happy that George calls on my bedchamber less frequently than of old. As is, I now endure but two calls a week, and when I hear his steps outside my door, I lie back on my bed, close my eyes and think of England.*
—LADY ALICE HILLINGDON, WIFE OF 2ND BARON HILLINGDON, 1912

At the turn of the century, respectable Englishwomen used to force themselves to think of their childbearing duty to the British Empire in order to get through any kind of passionate activity with an Englishman. Fast-forward a hundred years and there I was seduced by the mere thought of one day serving the British Empire! Trembling with pleasure at the very idea of passionate activity with an Englishman!

In my early twenties, I hit the town with dozens of British boys: boys with titles, boys descended from Winston Churchill, and boys who are now elected members of the Queen's government. I went out with racquets players, rugby players, wine merchants, Olympic rowers, Buckingham Palace staffers, and Rothschild bankers. I've been to weddings at Westminster Abbey and christenings at St. Paul's. I've had romantic moments that positively took my breath away and less than romantic moments that left me sobbing for weeks.

All of these Englishmen have been discussed and analyzed in excruciating detail with dozens of female friends via dozens of local and transatlantic phone calls. We've searched endlessly for evidence that might explain their behavior. All actions, all dialogue, all nuances have been examined repeatedly. Countless theories have been formed, but I'm sorry to say that I'm still working on a truly viable conclusion. The truth of the matter is that understanding the heart and mind of the English public-school boy can be more frustrating that the most grueling astrophysics course.

Still, with so many case studies at my fingertips, I've compiled some thoughts on the matter. This list certainly won't make the entire subject of Englishmen crystal clear, but whether your current infatuation is one of lasting love or passing lust—the following points might spare you unnecessary heartache or confusion and prepare you for the romantic pitfalls you will doubtlessly encounter. So without further ado . . .

## Here Is What I Know

1. Englishmen *like* American girls. They think we are cute, smart, and up for anything. They like hearing about cheerleading and sororities and what it's like to ride a yellow school bus and eat pancakes for breakfast. (That said, in the back of their minds, they are not sure if they can bring you home to

meet their parents. In the beginning, you are just an interesting experiment that happens to be good arm candy.)

2. **Boarding school messes them up a little.** When your mummy and daddy drop you off at a strange place when you're seven years old and only visit you three or four times a year for the next decade, it can't *not* damage you in some way. Abandonment issues? Definitely. Resentment? You better believe it. Emotional stunting? Affirmative. I'll never forget one tipsy evening when, in a moment of highly unusual candor, a handsome English boy explained to me that when his parents drove off that day and his little seven-year-old self realized he was never going to live at home again, it kind of *calcified* his heart. He actually used the word "calcified." There is a lot to be said for this, I think. British boarding school was invented to harden up young Englishmen in preparation for the great task of running the British Empire.* Even though such reasoning is no longer relevant, the assumed *necessity* of boarding school is an ideal the British upper middle classes still vehemently cling to. It's not that they are bad parents or don't love their children; it is simply *what is done*. Boarding school is assumed by their social set to be the finest English education—and it is precisely *because* they love their children and want the best for them that they swallow their tears, maintain a stiff upper lip, pack their little darlings up, and send them on their way. But you can't explain any of that to a first grader. Fast-forward twenty years and these poor British boys are still coming to

---

* Or, as written in the *London Times*, "to melt the boys down and make them all from the same mold like bullets."

terms with being left behind by those they loved most. As a coping mechanism, they tend to submerge any and all emotion. Their English hearts have already been through a lot, and initially, they can't bear to repeat such vulnerability by showing feelings for a girl. Besides, the way they see it, American girls have enough emotions for both of you, so why add more?

3. Englishmen are baffled by women because they grew up surrounded by men. Think about it: They're dropped off at their all-boys boarding school and spend the next ten years without a single female influence. Their peers are male, their teachers are male. In fact, most Englishmen of this social ilk really don't encounter girls at all until university. They are simultaneously awed by women and terrified of women—but they certainly don't come close to understanding women. Hence they decided long ago that the best way to cope with any and all female encounters is to get drunk.*

4. After eighteen years of life with no women, many adult Englishmen compensate by deciding never to be *without* women ever again. These boys *want* you around but have no clue how to *keep* you around. Don't take it personally because they literally are still learning. When Prince Charles infamously said, "Whatever 'in love' means," he wasn't being cruel toward Diana, he was simply being honest. He *genuinely* did not know what love was! Charles attended one of the harshest

---

* In my experience, British boys that have attended *co-ed* boarding schools or were sent away later in life (age thirteen or older) tend to be slightly more confident around women and/or not so emotionally repressed.

boarding schools in Britain (and as a child was made to shake hands with his mother rather than embrace her). Not all Englishmen are *this* emotionally repressed, but the fact remains that many crave the love they never felt and therefore have no idea how to express this strange feeling toward others. On the flip side, American girls are extremely in touch with their emotions (sometimes overly so), and while Englishmen find this refreshingly attractive, they also find it slightly petrifying because they have no idea how to appropriately reciprocate.

5. Because Englishmen are so emotionally closeted, big arguments rarely surface. Some girls think this is a plus. For me, the jury is out.

6. Englishmen have no idea what *dating* actually is. They've seen it happen in American movies, and when they pretend not to be watching *Sex and the City*. But it still confuses the hell out of them.

7. *Seeing other people?* What's that? *Exclusivity?* What's that? You must understand that these are *entirely American terms*. In England, you are in an instant monogamous relationship or you're indulging in a recreational night of passion—both are perfectly acceptable depending on what you're looking for—but you need to understand that to the male English brain, there is nothing in between.

8. Since debutante balls don't really exist anymore, English boys have to meet girls *somewhere*, and once they meet them they have to do *something* with them. So they make it up as they go along in that charming, bumbling, entirely inept way that epitomizes what it means to be English.

9. From the cradle to grave, British boys tend to mix within the same circle of friends. There is actually an embarrassment in certain English circles of introducing anyone to anyone, because of course everyone is supposed to know everyone already. In this bizarre insular world, it's best if you can make contact with an attractive English male through a mutual English friend or trusted English acquaintance. At least then the boy in question knows you are socially "safe."

10. If an introduction is not possible, and it often isn't because, after all, you only just moved to this crazy sceptered isle— then make sure the object of your affection is slightly under the influence. I'm not asking you to proactively spike his drinks, but all those English inhibitions and strict social protocols tend to evaporate after a few rounds of gin and tonics, so use this lubricated window to your advantage.

11. Ideally get him to approach you (Englishmen like to hunt— that's why they wear tweed). Make eye contact across the room. Smile demurely then lower your lashes à la Princess Diana. Repeat every thirty minutes.

12. When the moment is right, leave your group of friends and sit somewhere by yourself (pretend to check your messages or look for something in your bag). Or go to the bar and politely ask for a glass of water. As female prey, you are much more approachable (and less terrifying) if not surrounded by a gaggle of wing women.

13. When he finally says hello—and believe me, if he's drunk and you've been exchanging glances, eventually he will— play it cool. Keep smiling, keep laughing, and ask questions

(guys love to talk about themselves). You'll soon find that British guys have a rather seductive knack for turning even the smallest banalities into sparkling repartee.

14. Englishmen are attracted to our sincerity and openness, but don't scare him with loud Americanisms, bore him with silly things you don't like about England, or use any of the danger words that I mentioned in the section on language, (see page 40.)

15. Finish the drink in your hand as quickly as possible. When he asks if you'd like another (and he will), always accept. Drink this drink as slowly as possible.

16. If he asks you to dance, you may not be speaking to an actual Englishman! But if he is drunk enough, dancing could be in the cards, so don't be afraid to join him on the dance floor. I've found British boys to be surprisingly good dancers as long as you let them lead.

17. Try to leave the venue before he does. (I'm telling you, Cinderella knew what she was doing.) Place your business card in his hand and tell him to email you. Business cards are an excellent way to share your details without looking too forward or aggressive (and in many cases he won't have formally introduced himself or asked your name). When out and about in London, I *never* left the house without a small pack of cards in my purse. (If you don't have a business card, get a cute one made. It doesn't have to have an actual business on it. If the Victorians did it, so can you.)

18. The majority of Englishmen don't have the social skills to ask for your number. Don't take this personally. It just

doesn't occur to them as the obvious next step in seeing you again.

19. If he miraculously remembers to ask for your number, and you actually want to see him again—give it to him! (And, come on—if you don't trust him with your number, why are you still standing there talking to him?)

20. Rather than reciting your number to him, suggest calling him from your phone so your number appears on his screen. This is a coy way of getting his digits and putting you on an equal playing field—because god knows it can be hellish if he has your number and you don't have his.

21. Kiss him good-bye on the cheek (or if you dare, on the lips) and make a quick exit. Text later that evening—something short, sweet, and flirty but not overly sexual. Then, however excruciating it may be, resist all urges to make contact again. The ball is officially in his court.

22. Sometimes the evening gets carried away and you are way past kissing on the cheek. He'll offer to share a cab home with you, but mainly because he's hoping to be invited in. Please keep in mind that all Englishmen are NSIT!

23. If you really want to see him again, avoid staying the night at his flat. Even if you come in for, in the words of my friend Olivia, "a quick drink and a fumble," call a cab to take you home at three in the morning. It's so much classier (and so much more mysterious) than waking up with panda eyes in last night's party clothes.

24. If you simply got drunk and accidently spent the night with him, don't panic. Englishmen seem to be fond of what I call

"reverse dating"—meaning it is very common for dinner and a movie to happen *after* your first sexual encounter (this is especially true for university students).

25. If you haven't heard from him after a week or so, ask mutual friends to do some sleuthing for you and/or push him in the right direction. Sometimes a little nudge is all it takes.

26. Unfortunately, there are times when you simply won't hear from him ever again. You can't take this personally. The magical chemistry you felt during your first encounter *was* real (don't try to convince yourself otherwise), it's just that most Englishmen lack the skills to hold on to it. Don't be angry with him; just be amused at his ineptitude. (And remember that when it comes to matters of the heart, he's probably been through just as much pain as you have—but being English, he has absolutely no clue how to deal with it.)

27. Nine times out of ten, when he *does* finally contact you—an Englishman will text, not call. These texts are usually vague, often funny, and will always require some degree of decrypting.

28. Don't expect to be asked out immediately. (See numbers 3, 4, and 6.) In the beginning, if he fancies you—he will simply try to make you laugh.

29. Texting and email technologies are actually a dream come true for most Englishmen—both allow British boys to avoid verbalizing any type of emotion while facilitating their innate love of language and wordplay. Emails and

text messages give Englishmen the courage and the platform to say all kinds of things to a girl that they wouldn't dream of saying to her in person. That blinking cursor magically negates many of their deep-seated English inhibitions, and in fact, I sometimes think that when it comes to romantic interaction, for British men, it's very similar to being drunk.

30. Don't reply to his messages immediately. Make him wait. Make him worry and wonder if you will reply at all. (The only exception to this is late night texting, which tends to be more flirtatious and move at a faster pace.)

31. When he does suggest meeting up again, don't expect a well-thought-out evening (and don't expect him to pick you up). In all reality, he'll probably just invite you to a pub that is convenient for him. It doesn't mean he doesn't like you or he doesn't want to spend time with you—it just simply never occurred to him to make reservations at a restaurant.

32. Englishmen specialize in what I call the "non-date date"—which means don't be surprised if his friends are already there when you arrive, or if his friends show up halfway into the evening. (Warning: He will seem slightly more relaxed in the company of his friends, but slightly less doting toward you. He may also forget to introduce you to them.) Don't take any of this personally. It is just how British boys do things.

33. You'll probably be expected to drink all evening without eating. (Again, this doesn't mean he doesn't like you or he

doesn't want to spend time with you—it just simply never occurred to him to make reservations at a restaurant.)

34. If it's just the two of you—and he invited you out, he pays for the drinks. It's that simple. Don't overthink it any more than this. (If his friends are there, offering to buy a round is always a nice gesture.)

35. Playing hard to get in itself can be hard, so in the beginning, only agree to dates (or non-date dates) on school nights. That way you have an excellent excuse not to go home with him.

36. If you actually find yourself sitting with an actual Englishman at an actual restaurant with menus—then give yourself a pat on the back. This means you have an unusual English specimen. You have an Englishman who not only thinks he feels (yikes!) *an emotion* toward you, but is familiar with the concept of dating and, even more so, the concept of a dinner date. He's not entirely sure what happens on these "dates," but he knows that they usually happen at restaurants. This is *huge* evolutionary progress.

37. Try to put the poor guy at ease. Make breezy American chit-chat. Tell him what you think looks good on the menu (so he doesn't worry that you're ordering lobster). And for your sake and his, order a bottle of wine asap.

38. Keeping your new continental table manners in the forefront of your mind, order food that you feel confident eating the correct way. And even if you're on a low-carb diet, I need you to eat at least one piece of bread—not only to prac-

tice your bread plate skills but to soak up all those glasses of wine.

39. Laugh at yourself. Don't take yourself too seriously. There is nothing that puts British men at ease more than irony, self-deprecation, and humor.

40. Smile a lot and ask him questions that aren't too intrusive. (Don't forget that most Brits are reserved, intensely private creatures and will recoil at any attempt to make them talk about their feelings.)

41. Unless you are waxing lyrical about (a) the monarchy or (b) your dog—try to avoid overly emotional subjects of any kind. (Your views on foxhunting and astrology should also wait till at least the third or fourth date.)

42. Avoid sounding like you're interviewing him for a job—least of all a job called "husband." Asking him about his favorite cities in the world is great; asking questions about his net worth or if he wants kids? Not so great.

43. Even if his accent is making you go weak at the knees (and let's be honest, it probably is) try to control yourself. Don't ask him to say certain words just so you can listen to his voice (English guys eventually find this rather tiresome)—instead try to concentrate on what he's actually saying.

44. After dessert, strategically time your visit to the ladies' room so you are not at the table when the bill arrives. This will allow him to pay without any awkwardness. When you return to the table, thank him graciously and reiterate how much you enjoyed the meal. (British men often tell me that

American women are so much more appreciative than English girls, and they love that about us.)

45. If a trip to the loo is not possible, and the bill is placed between you, stay calm. (If you start acting awkward, he'll act even more awkward.) But the same rule remains: If he invited you out, he pays. Don't overthink it.*

46. I don't care if you're a modern woman who earns twice as much as he does; splitting the bill is the universal sign of disinterest, and subconsciously, guys find it emasculating. So only offer to go Dutch if you've decided you never want to see him again.

47. After dinner you will probably meet up with his friends for more drinking, or he will suggest it's time to be getting home. Don't be offended by either—you'll still get a kiss at the end of the night. If he invites you to his flat for "a coffee," it's more than a coffee that's on offer.

48. Most Englishmen are either deathly afraid of a monogamous relationship (see number 3) or they literally can't make it through their day-to-day life unless they are in what they *think* is a monogamous relationship (see number 4). Because American-style dating falls somewhere in between and his English brain can't compute it, he will make up his mind one way or the other and he will do so quite quickly. So quickly it can seem (a) disingenuous or (b) brutal—depending on which option he chooses. I can't tell you how many times I've

---

* Sometimes reaching toward your handbag in search of your wallet is a nice gesture. But when he insists on paying, don't argue with him.

gone out with a British guy *twice* and after the second encounter was (a) assumed by his friends and family to be his
new and permanent girlfriend and invited to weddings, family vacations, and Christmas, or (b) he seemingly dropped off
the face of the earth, and I never heard from him ever again.
(See "Alien Abduction," page 217.) Both situations are baf-
fling, but that's just how it seems to work.

49. Englishmen are good kissers, and contrary to popular belief,
they are good at other things as well.

50. I know plenty of American girls who have married British boys. They don't all have titles or live in castles, but
I want you to know that it *does* happen. Despite all the
legal, linguistic, cultural, geographical, and psychosomatic
obstacles—occasionally love prevails.

*A curious background surely for a kiss*
*Our first—Westminster Bridge at break of day—*
*Settings by Wordsworth, as John used to say.*
—FROM *THE WHITE CLIFFS* BY ALICE DUER MILLER

5 LONDON KISSES AMERICAN GIRLS MUST EXPERIENCE BEFORE THEY DIE:

1. In the back of a black cab

2. On a moving escalator beneath a tube station (Holborn is the longest—but *please* stand on the *right*!)

3. Walking along the South Bank

4. On the back of a Trafalgar Square lion in the moonlight

5. Westminster Brinde at dawn

# Texting

The Englishmen's desire to cling to technology while dating can be infuriating. There were several times when I genuinely felt as if my entire relationship was limited to the words that fit onto a one-inch-by-one-inch screen, and occasionally I was forced to ask myself how long I could be sustained on fewer than five abbreviated sentences per week (which for some nonverbal British males is more than enough communication for the month). So my advice to you is this: Texting is fine, as long as you have face time to go with it.

RULES FOR TEXTING:

- In an age of iPhones, BlackBerrys, and predictive text, there is no excuse for lazy abbreviations and tacky acronyms. No matter what the medium, always use the Queen's English.

- Certain social circles believe that abbreviation of any kind implies that you are busy—and this is the worst possible label to incur, as it also implies that you are not a gentleman or lady of leisure. Unlike the working classes, true ladies who lunch have time to spell out every word of their text messages.

- Signing your texts with your name or initial plus an x is quite normal. (For example, I often sign off "Jx"). The x implies an affectionate, sometimes flirtatious, sometimes loving kiss— and should only be used when you want to show affection, flirtation, or love to the recipient. Men only use x's when messaging their mothers, girlfriends, or potential girlfriends. Women use x's when messaging absolutely everyone except strangers, female coworkers they don't particularly like, or male coworkers they have no desire to flirt with. (The same x etiquette applies to email correspondence.)

*The American girl has the advantage of her English*
*sister in that she possesses all that the other lacks.*
—FROM *TITLED AMERICANS*, 1890

## Online Dating

Transatlantic matches were such the rage during the Gilded Age that American girls were known to consult a quarterly publication called *Titled Americans*. This magazine contained a register of all the eligible, titled British bachelors on the market, with a handy description listing their age, accomplishments, and prospects. The journal described itself as a "carefully composed list of peers who are eager to lay their coronets and their hearts at the feet of the all-conquering American girl." But basically it was the nineteenth-century version of Match.com.

As you know, the taboo on meeting someone over the Internet has completely disappeared for our generation, and this applies to both sides of the Atlantic. Sparks may not fly with every encounter, but with London social barriers being what they are, don't turn your nose up to a technology that might, at the very least, lead you to some new English friends (who in turn might introduce you to someone with whom sparks *will* fly!). So I wholeheartedly urge you to give it a try.

Unfortunately *Titled Americans* is no longer in existence. Nevertheless, I encourage you to check out www.datebritishguys.com. They claim to provide love-hungry American women with single British men who live in the UK (and the US). Believe me, if this genius of a site had been around when I was single, I would have logged on in a heartbeat.

Old standbys like Match.com and DatingDirect are also widely used by guys in London, so don't be afraid to widen your net and post your profile on more than one site. If your politics are left-leaning, try Guardian Soulmates; if you tend to be more conservative, try Telegraph Dating (though the latter tends to attract an older crowd).

# Parable # 6

When I first ventured into the heady world of online dating, I saw no point in trawling through hundreds of undesirables, so as I composed my profile, I was certain to be specific about what I was looking for. After a handful of drafts, I settled on this:

*Blonde American bookworm/partygirl seeks privately educated Englishman (aged 25–30) with James Bond accent and Oscar Wilde wit. Must enjoy black-tie galas, debaucherous dinner parties, intellectual debates, and long walks in the country. An appreciation for fine wine, classic literature, and nonstop adventure goes without saying. Aristocratic lineage and Hugh Grant looks highly encouraged. No others need apply.*

Once it was posted, I sat back and waited for the flirty fun to begin. Eventually I began corresponding with an Oxford graduate named Sebastian who listed art history, French literature, and fencing as his hobbies and claimed to be the CEO of his own company as well as writing a novel in his spare time. We exchanged pictures (he was preppy and cute with classic aquiline features) and agreed to meet for a drink the following week. When he suggested my favorite London bar, I got goose bumps, and it wasn't long before I became a nervous wreck. I mean, this guy seemed *amazing*. What if I wasn't good enough for him? What if I wasn't pretty enough? What if I wasn't smart enough?

I went to the bookstore and bought the cheater's guides to French literature and art history. I also read everything I could get my hands on about fencing. During the next few days, I ignored my work entirely and spent hours composing note-perfect paragraphs in response to Sebastian's seductively cerebral emails.

My heart raced wildly with every email exchange, and my stomach filled with endless butterflies at the thought of our pending date. But as I walked into the dimly lit bar situated ten storeys above the sparkling lights of the River Thames, I knew—within seconds—that I shouldn't have bothered.

There was zero chemistry between us. Not a spark of physical attraction. Not even enough basic compatibility to sustain thirty minutes of small talk. Although our email discussions had flown off the keyboard at lightning speed, we struggled to make a simple face-to-face conversation last as long as a single glass of wine.

On the lonely taxi ride home, I marveled at my heart's gullibility. I couldn't believe I had let myself get so worked up! To become so emotionally involved! So unsure of myself! To think I was devouring French literature in order to impress him! *He* should have been devouring things to impress *me*!

TIPS FOR ONLINE DATING:

- Don't change your criteria just because an entire e-pool of men has opened up before you. Stay strict about what you're looking for and refer to my aforementioned Castle Crew guidelines. You won't be able to hear his accent over an email, so at the very least make sure he went to an appropriate British boarding school or university.

- Witty in an email does not mean witty in real life. Not all Englishmen are natural raconteurs, but well-written emails can give them the appearance of being so.

- Do not exchange emails for more than a week or you'll become more emotionally attached to him (or, more accurately, emotionally attached to who you think he is) than you realize.

&bull; Have confidence in yourself and arrange to meet up as soon as possible. That way, if sparks don't fly, you haven't wasted too much time or invested too much of your heart and soul.

&bull; Agree to meet for a drink (not dinner) so you have the option of leaving early if he's not your type. (This only backfires when the guy orders a second bottle of wine while you're in the loo and you are forced to politely consume several more glasses on an empty stomach before you can make your exit. Yes, I speak from experience.)

&bull; Occasionally sparks *do* fly! I've been to five weddings (and counting) of couples who met online. I have no doubt there will be more to come.

# Alien Abduction

Let's say you've been dating (and non-dating) an Englishman for several weeks. Things seem to be going well—he is affectionate, complimentary, and flirty every time you see him; you have met a smattering of his friends; you've seen each other's flats (with the occasional sleepover); and you genuinely seem to be having fun in each other's company. You might be sleeping together, you might not be, but in any case you've made plans to go to the cinema next Friday night.

In the week that follows, he doesn't call you, but you shrug it off assuming he is busy. All of your texts to him are met with one-word answers, but you don't think much of it. But then Thursday night rolls around and you still haven't heard from him. On Friday afternoon he might (*might!*) text you with a cryptic explanation like "something came up." That's the good scenario.

The bad scenario involves no text warning whatsoever and he simply drops off the face of the earth, never to be heard from again. Total radio silence.

For all you know he's really and truly been abducted by aliens, but whatever the reason he simply vanishes from your life. In the course of my London dating career, this happened to me at least four or five times. (It may actually have happened to me more than this, but for my own sanity, I stopped counting.) This same pattern has also happened to dozens of girlfriends of mine—both English and American.

So what is the deal? Why are these aliens selfishly abducting so many of our beloved Englishmen? I'm not entirely sure. I'm simply not willing to believe that all English guys are bastards. Nor am I willing to believe (mainly because it's just too depressing) that English guys are going to put in all that long-term romantic effort for the sake of a few make-out sessions if all along they have secret plans to escape to the mother ship.

So here is my theory: As with all things in their lives, Englishmen do what they think is expected of them. Their peers, their parents, and their entire social class and structure expect them to engage in some kind of courtship with a girl that will eventually lead to a serious and permanent relationship. Most Englishmen have no idea how to go about doing this (or have any idea if they even *want* to be doing this), but nevertheless they maintain a stiff upper lip and do their best to meet everyone's expectations—including yours.

Dating is awkward for them because in reality they are just going through the motions, and they haven't quite figured out that *real* courtship requires genuine passion, honest emotions, and a certain level of informality and spontaneity—all of which are qualities that are entirely un-English.

Still, he does what he *thinks* he should do and acts how he *thinks* he should act and is extremely charming and polite while doing so. He *thinks* he should make you feel beautiful and special, so he does just that (and happens to do it in a devastating accent that makes you melt into a puddle on the floor). He *thinks* he should act like a perfect gentleman, so he does. Meanwhile, you don't have a hope in hell. Of course you're going to fall for him!

I mean, based on his behavior, he seems seriously interested in you—so you begin to reciprocate. That's when the Englishman starts to panic. He is officially in over his head and starts sending frantic SOS alarm signals to the mother ship. He clearly can't tell you what he is feeling—that would involve (a) admitting feelings, (b) verbalizing feelings, and (c) confrontation—all of which are unthinkable for an English male. Instead, he thinks it's best if he just disappears for a while and pretends the whole thing never happened. It's around now that you start wondering why you haven't heard from him in more than a week.

In some cases, you will hear from him six months later through Facebook. It will be some cute, neutral, sometimes flirtatious message just to see "how you are" or "what you're up to." It's his inept English way of admitting that he's behaved badly, absolving his guilt, and clearing the air in case your paths cross again through mutual friends. He sends this message not necessarily because he wants to, but because he *thinks he should.*

I must reiterate that alien abductions are by no means the norm, but I feel it is my duty to warn my American sisters of their existence. And while alien abductions can be painful—I firmly believe that they can't be nearly as painful as going through life never having dated an Englishman.

# Winning Him Back

Whenever my particular Englishman of the moment was abducted by aliens, I was confused and devastated (and often genuinely heartbroken)—but more than anything I was convinced that I could use my feminine wiles to win him back.

I made this mistake time and time again before it finally dawned on me to stop giving my heart to one English guy after another—when they clearly hadn't asked for it. If an Englishman pulls back and retreats to his mother ship, he is not engaging in the mythical tactic known as "treat 'em mean, keep 'em keen"—it is genuinely because he is simply not ready for a grown-up relationship.

For years, I point-blank refused to believe this. So I busied myself with all kinds of harebrained strategies to make these British boys see the light, to make them realize that the mother ship was *not* where they wanted to be. I thought if they only realized *how much* I cared for them, then they would automatically decide to care for me in return. Most of the time, my efforts failed, and I only felt further rejected. But sometimes, my flirty texts or well-timed Facebook messages would pay off and he'd actually ask to see me again. But this scenario was almost worse, because deep down, I knew that I had not won him back, I had just temporarily outsmarted him! And deep down, who wants a guy that you have to trick into going out with you?

I'll never forget the moment when the above epiphany occurred to me. It was almost midnight on a Sunday and I was sitting in my tiny London bedroom, painting my nails seashell pink—when the thought just popped into my brain: *If a guy doesn't want to be with me, it's because he is not the right guy for me.*

Let me tell you, the sheer clarity of it nearly knocked me over.

And from that day on, my English dating life changed. Because I finally realized that when love isn't in our lives, it's because *true love* is on its way.

## RECOMMENDED READING:

### *Bridget Jones's Diary* by Helen Fielding

Yes, the movie stars Hugh Grant at his devilish best, but I promise you the book is even better. This book *defined* the literary genre of brainy yet batty girls wandering through London looking for Mr. Right yet always falling for Mr. Wrong. Fielding is the Nancy Mitford of our generation, and as far as I'm concerned *Bridget Jones's Diary* is such a classic that it belongs on every English syllabus. If you're dating, or attempting to date, English guys, you must, must read it.

### *Mr. Maybe* by Jane Green

This highly relatable London novel depicts the eternal dilemma that all girls face at one point: Do you choose the impoverished guy that you're head-over-heels in love with or the super-successful guy that's in love with you? When all the titles and castles and jewels get to your head, this book is a wonderful reminder of what's really important when it comes to matters of the heart.

### *Enchanted Love* by Marianne Williamson

I read *a lot* of new age, self-help books during my roller-coaster single years, and a lot of them were useless. But somehow this book managed to cut through the jargon and speak to my very soul. Marianne's words and affirmations gave me a new perspective regarding the search for love—and the meaning of love—and totally changed my approach to men, relationships, and dating in general. I was in tears as I read some chapters, but because of this book, I learned to stop some heartwrenching patterns in my love life. Whether you live in London or not, you should read this book. It truly is enchanting.

# EIGHT

# FAKE IT TILL YOU
# MAKE IT

*The poor man is not he who is without a cent,*
*but he who is without a dream.*

—HARRY KEMP

A n American friend of mine named Max once told me that living with London's ludicrously high prices was "kind of like living without a limb"—not ideal or especially pleasant, but eventually you kind of adjust. As weird as it is, this is the best analogy on the subject I've ever heard.

I'm not going to lie to you. London *is* expensive. Very. But you know what? So is college. So are weddings. So are houses. So are kids. And somehow people manage to get through all those stages in life just fine. Yes, sometimes you might have to decide between buying a fantastic Burberry* raincoat and eating lunch for a month.

---

* However, you must never buy anything with the Burberry pattern as that now has very lower-class connotations; play it safe with a classic Macintosh trench coat.

But believe me when I tell you that living in London will nourish you in its own way.

I'm a girl with very expensive tastes (I can't help it, I was born that way). When I came to London, I had zero money but was hardly going to let a meager income cramp my style. I abhorred the idea of conforming to any kind of boring sounding "budget"—but the day I had to turn down a date with a cute British boy because I couldn't afford to get my highlights done was the day I knew I had better start getting my finances under control. And what I eventually discovered was that a little bit of money with a bunch of creativity is *way* more amusing than a bunch of money with zero creativity. (At least that's what I'll keep telling myself until I finally move into my very own castle.)

So even though everything in London costs roughly four times more than it should (I'm not joking; a bottle of water is like $8), there are ways to save if you know what you're doing.

## Fashion & Grooming

There are no walk-in closets in London, so most Brits make do with a small wooden "wardrobe" crammed into the corner of their already small bedroom. My husband often comments that my wardrobe looks like something in a cartoon because it is literally bursting with items of clothing. ("Do you need me to help you fold some of that?" he often asks me—he was made to fold all his clothes with military standards while at boarding school and apparently some habits never die.) But I never get rid of anything because I actually *wear everything*! And the fact that I never tire of my clothes is proof of their inherent rightness.

So here are my tips—because believe me, the one thing worse than *being* broke is *looking* broke . . .

🐚 Conviction and poise come cheap. Your wardrobe does not have to be expensive or contain a single designer label as long as you wear what you have with confidence and grace—both of which cost nothing.

🐚 Never buy anything unless you LOVE it. When you don't have much money, you should only buy clothing that compels you to press your nose against the shop window and drool.

🐚 Shop in America. As mentioned before, I recommend hitting the US sales every time you go home. Clothes in America are at least *30 percent cheaper* than in the UK,* and you will have the added bonus of owning items no one else in London has.

🐚 Buy classic, timeless pieces. I *still* wear things that I bought nearly fifteen years ago, and everything in my wardrobe works just as well now as it did a half a century ago. I wear bejeweled cardigans that my grandmother wore in her *Mad Men* years; I wear my mother's pleated skirts that she wore in Paris when she was thirteen years old. "Fashion" is forever in a state of flux, but classics stay in style forever. (There is no

---

* Even stores that exist in both the US and UK—like Banana Republic—are much more expensive on the other side of the pond. When I found out BR was coming to London, I was so happy that I nearly threw a party. Then I saw their pricing: a tank top that costs $25 in the US costs £25 (or $40) in the UK.

better example of this than Her Majesty the Queen—HM refuses to submit to the tyranny of fashion trends and never deviates from her fabulous 1950s style.)

- Buy quality. Chinese cashmere is cheaper that Scottish cashmere but will start pilling within weeks. Throwaway fashion from trendy, but scarily cheap stores will be unwearable in a couple of months, not only because the items will literally be falling apart at the seams, but what were once "must have" fashion pieces according to *British Vogue* now look ridiculous. Buying well-made clothing is better for the environment, better for children in sweatshops, better for your wallet, and better for your wardrobe—everybody wins.

- Take care of your clothes. Yes, my tiny closet if filled to the brim, but I always use padded hangers (never metal) and my sweaters are always stored with protective mothballs.

- Allow yourself to purchase one new fashion item per month—no more, no less. Spend as much as you reasonably can to ensure quality fabric and quality workmanship. If you always choose timeless pieces, you'll know you will have them for years to come, and if you divide the cost of the item by how many times you will wear it—it's always a bargain. Compare this to any cheap catwalk-inspired item that you will stop wearing after a month, and the savings are astronomical.

- Check eBay. If you see something you like in a shop but it's too expensive—look for it on eBay. I've bought several brand-new items from J.Crew and L.K. Bennett this way, and the discount is substantial.

◈ Look in the kids' department. If you're not too tall, children's clothing can be a savvy saver's dream (e.g., an adult raincoat from Burberry is $1,000; the girl's size 16 Burberry raincoat is $350).

◈ In Chapter 3, I mentioned the best London shops for finding classic wardrobe pieces (see page 78)—these stores can be pricey, but the craftsmanship is worth every penny. However, if you are craving some British retail therapy and need something more affordable, I suggest browsing through:
*Joules* (colorful, preppy casuals), www.joules.com
*Massimo Dutti* (a Spanish brand with a Ralph Lauren feel), www.massimodutti.com

◈ Do your own nails. English nail salons are atrociously expensive and their standards are subpar. You're much better off buying a few bottles of nude or clear polish (I like Essie "Sugar Daddy"—it's very similar to the shade Kate Middleton wore at her engagement photo call)—and taking ten minutes to paint them yourself twice a week. Same applies to your toes (I like Essie "Bordeaux"—the perfect shade of vintage red). Don't forget to finish with a clear top coat. Not only will your nails look better than any you'll see on 99 percent of British women—you'll save about $150 a week! (You can always treat yourself to a professional mani-pedi when you go back to America.)

◈ When it comes to hair, I follow the same rule I use for nails— if you can, get it done in the US. However, sometimes a girl just can't wait around for a family wedding as an excuse to go back to America and get her highlights done. Still, I suggest waiting as long as you possibly can between each visit to the salon. If you get fewer, thicker highlights, they'll look more natural when the roots begin to show, not to mention that using fewer chemicals is healthier for your hair. I've been to what seems like a *billion* London salons seeking out a colorist whom I trust with my tresses, and I finally found a color team that I can safely recommend: Four London, www .fourlondon.com. They're based in Mayfair, and the business is owned and operated entirely by women. They do such a great job I only need to go four times a year. PS: Tipping £5–10 is perfectly fine.

## London Transportation

*Parking your car in London costs more than the minimum wage. There are people in London working in McDonald's who can look out their windows and see parking meters earning more than they do.*
—SIMON EVANS

The good news is that you absolutely don't need a car to live in London. Considering that I endured more than sixty hellish hours of UK driving lessons and failed my UK driving test three times before finally passing, this is actually *fantastic* news. (Even still, the last time I got behind the wheel on the wrong side of the road was the day I passed this aforementioned test.) It will shock you how fast you get over not having a car in your life (and how long it will take you to stop getting into a car on the wrong side).

## The Tube

London has a wonderful public transport system. Unlike the subway system in Manhattan (which scares the hell out of me), the London Underground (aka "the tube") is clean, well lit, safe, and easy to understand for people like me who are terrible at reading maps. However, the tube map is not at all to scale, and going underground throws things way out of proportion. (For weeks I was changing trains at Queensway to get to Bayswater when all I had to do was walk ten seconds down the street to get from one to the other.) So when you first arrive in London, try to walk the city as much as you can to get a feel for how the various neighborhoods connect. (But don't forget to look *left* when crossing the street!)

NOTE: If you travel five days a week, it is significantly cheaper to buy an annual travel card rather than a daily, weekly, or monthly ticket—most employers will loan you the cash up front. You also receive a significant discount if you are a full-time student.

I love commuting by tube, because the people watching is *amazing*, and unlike driving, which requires exhausting mental concentration, the tube allows you to read or sleep on the way to work. My only advice would be to bring a bottle of water with you on a hot day, have some ballet flats in your bag in case you don't get a seat, and depending on what time you commute, prepare to get up close and personal. (My friend often jokes that personal space in England simply means that someone is not standing *on* you.) Always let passengers get off the train before you get on, and *always* give up your seat to the elderly, the pregnant, and the disabled. Don't panic when they announce over the intercom that there is "a body under the train." Apparently, there is at least one suicide per day on the London train network (I blame all that gray weather)—when this fact annoys you more than it disturbs you, you have officially become a true Londoner.

The tube is also a great venue for feasting your eyes on cute boys. (As ever, keep your eyes peeled for gold signet rings.) That said, I'm head over heels in love with a new website—it's nothing short of pure genius, and I'm not afraid to say that I vote almost weekly: http://tubecrush.net/. Here you can view page after fantastic page of English guys going about their daily lives—totally unaware of the joy they are bringing to their fellow passengers.

## The Bus

Taking the bus is even cheaper than taking the tube and only slightly more difficult to navigate. (Many commuters prefer the bus because they can gaze out the window at London's beautiful scenery rather than gaze across the aisle at the tube's eclectic passengers.) And you haven't lived until you've experienced a London night bus at least once—sometimes they are parties all unto themselves.

Note: The number 11 bus is excellent for sightseeing and much cheaper than the "official" red tour buses.

## Taxis

I believe that it was Jerry Seinfeld who quipped that the only qualification required to become a New York taxi driver is a face. This is not the case for London taxis. You will find that London black cabs are things of beauty—they are clean, have plenty of headroom, all the doors are attached, they can hold up to five people, the drivers always speak English, and—get this—the drivers always know exactly where they are going. This is because all licensed London taxi drivers must pass a test called "The Knowledge" before they are allowed to work behind the wheel. They must *memorize* 320 routes in and around the capital, as well as all the landmarks and places of interest along these routes. They actually pride themselves on not needing maps—that's how good they are. The downside is that cabs (especially at night) are expensive. To save money, after a big night out, arrange to split the fare with your friends, and if you don't all live in the same area, take turns sleeping over at one another's flat. It's cheaper, and compared to drunkenly venturing home by yourself at three in the morning, it's also safer.

Always emerge from a taxi (or any car for that matter) with your knees together, bringing your legs from the car to the pavement in one swift, graceful motion.

## Mini Cabs

Do not get into any unlicensed "mini cab"—these drivers will come up to you, point to a normal-looking car, and try to offer you a cheap ride home. When you're drunk and tired (and broke), taking them up on their offer can be really tempting—but please don't risk it. Don't get into a car with a stranger! A safer option is to prearrange a *licensed* mini cab to pick you up at the end of the night—not only are they cheaper than black cabs, but no hailing is required, because they will be waiting for you when you tumble out the nightclub door.

My favorite mini cab company is Green Tomato Cars, www .greentomatocars.com. Their fleet is made up entirely of eco-friendly hybrids. It's nice to know that after hours of damaging your liver, at least you're not damaging the environment on the way home.

# Going Out

*It is not what we have but what we enjoy*
*that constitutes our abundance.*
—JOHN PETIT-SENN

In my twenties I made very little money (not to mention I had a mountain of student loans to pay off). Still, every Thursday, Friday, and Saturday night, my friend Hattie and I would head straight to London's most fashionable nightspots, stroll confidently up to the bar in our best high heels, and order a glass of champagne as if we were dazzling London socialites . . .

HOW TO HAVE A FULL NIGHT ON AN ALMOST EMPTY WALLET:

- When it came to nights out in London, my friend Hattie and I had a pact: We would each buy one round of drinks (which meant two drinks each). After that, if guys hadn't offered to buy us a third drink, we would call it a night, save our money and go home. (Lucky for us, we never had to go home.) I'm categorically *not* advising you to prostitute yourself for a free martini—but if you're single and looking for flirtatious fun, there is no point in buying all your own drinks when London is full of cute boys who are perfectly happy and able to buy them for you.

- I'm a big proponent of pre-drinking. I'm not suggesting you arrive at the bar/club slurring, but having an affordable glass (or two) of wine at home means you won't require expensive cocktails later in the evening. (Note: This only works if you pre-drink in moderation; otherwise you will be too drunk to care if you are buying expensive cocktails later in the evening.)

🔊 Go to every single party you are invited to. Drinks (and sometimes canapés) are free, and you never know where the evening will lead you. It was not uncommon for me to go to a house party, a bar, and a members club in a single evening without paying for a single alcoholic beverage.

🔊 When you *are* buying the drinks, order drinks without mixers (a flute of champagne, a glass of good wine, a classic martini) for the simple reason that strong, pure drinks last longer. All those fruity cocktails are kind of silly anyway—teach yourself to appreciate the grown-up taste of real liquor— the iciness of imported vodka, the smokiness of single malt scotch, the creaminess of bourbon. Even better, learn to love a perfectly mixed martini.

🔊 Be thankful for London's licensing laws. American bars make it all too easy to keep drinking through the night— even if you have to get up for work in the morning. But most pubs and bars in London stop serving alcohol at 11 p.m. This may sound like a downer, but it's actually a great excuse to catch the last train home,* get some sleep, stop spending money, and not roll into the office with a hangover. If it's Friday or Saturday night, you'll probably want to continue the revelry at another club or late night bar—but at least "last

---

* From central London, the tube stops running approximately thirty minutes after midnight.

orders" allows you to stop and reassess your evening, meaning there is less of a chance of accidently staying out till two in the morning.

- Never go home with a boy to save money on cab fare. I actually know of girls who have done this, and I think it's ridiculous. Go home with a boy for any silly reason you want—just don't make it an economic one.

- Go to the theater! London boasts one of the best theater scenes in the world (many plays start here before heading to Broadway), and getting last-minute standby tickets is surprisingly easy, not to mention one of the better bargains in the city. Personally, I love getting cheap "box seats"—the view is only slightly restricted and you get to sit exactly where the royals were sitting less than a hundred years ago. Of course while I'm up there, I occasionally wave to my "subjects," pretending that nothing has changed.

- Stay in at least three nights a week—that way you can't spend money even if you want to. My chosen nights were Sunday, Monday, and Tuesday. Even if I was invited out on these nights, I'd refuse or suggest we reschedule. If it was something I couldn't possibly turn down, I'd make myself stay in on Wednesday or Thursday to compensate. Not only were these nights my money-saving nights, they were my *healthy* nights. I'd go to the gym, I'd have a big (cheap) salad for dinner, and not a drop of alcohol would pass my lips.

- Acquire a GBF (gay best friend) or two. They are always good-looking, always intelligent, and always successful—and you can always count on them to buy you dinner. The downside is you can't marry them.

# Martinis: James Bond–Style

*"A dry martini," Bond said. "One.*
*In a deep champagne goblet."*
*"Oui, monsieur."*
*"Three measures of Gordon's,*
*one of vodka, half a measure of Kina Lillet.*
*Shake it very well until it's ice-cold,*
*then add a large thin slice of lemon peel. Got it?"*
—FROM *CASINO ROYALE* BY IAN FLEMING

If you have only one drink per evening, make it a martini. Martinis are ingenious inventions when you think about it. There is simply no other way to down large quantities of neat liquor without looking like a tramp. But pour the fiery concoction into a martini glass? Suddenly drinking straight gin becomes chic and stylish. To the inexperienced palate, it may taste a bit like lighter fluid, but it looks beautiful in the glass and you feel elegant holding it.

It is widely believed that the best martinis in the world are served at London's Dukes Hotel—a luxuriously discreet building tucked behind Clarence House and St. James's Palace. It was at Dukes that James Bond author Ian Fleming came to drink and where Bond's famous preference to have his martini "shaken, not stirred" was born. (Apparently this request is highly unusual, because shaking the ice actually waters down the drink and alters the flavor of the liquor.)

Since the first Bond film in 1962, all of the 007s (including the dashing Sean Connery, Roger Moore, Pierce Brosnan, and Daniel Craig) have frequented the Dukes Bar.

Her Majesty the Queen has been known to attend private parties at Dukes (she likes it there because it's near her house), the late

Princess of Wales often came in for tea, and Prince Edward likes to stop by when he's in the neighborhood. If you want to rub shoulders with royalty, get yourself out of those wet London clothes and into a dry martini. www.dukeshotel.com/

While a single Dukes martini will last you all night,* you can easily make your own.

Here is their world-famous recipe:

### *The Dukes Classic Martini*

1. Both the bottles and the glasses should be kept in the freezer.
2. Use premium alcohol only: Smirnoff Black vodka and Bombay Sapphire, Tanqueray, or Greenall's gin.
3. Splash one drop of Martini Bianco (dry) into a frosted martini glass.
4. Add two large measures of gin or vodka.
5. Cut a 4 centimeter chunk of peel from a lemon. Do not twist it. Instead, snap the peel in half lengthwise, wipe it slowly around the rim of the glass, then slide it into the alcohol. Enjoy.

## Frugal Foodies

Contrary to popular belief, you don't have to spend a lot to eat well in London. Here are some of my favorite cheap and cheerful places that offer good food and a fun atmosphere at very affordable prices.

---

* "I never have more than one drink before dinner. But I do like that one to be large and very strong and very cold and very well-made." —James Bond (*Casino Royale*)

- *The Giraffe Café*. Happy, healthy eating. Great salads, burgers, and cheesecake. www.giraffe.net

- *Nando's Chicken*. Portuguese style peri-peri flame-grilled chicken with all the trimmings. Very spicy! Very affordable. www.nandos.co.uk

- *Busaba Eathai*. Trendy atmosphere, very affordable, and always delicious. (Try the crab pad Thai and the ginger calamari!) www.busaba.com

- *Wagamama Noodle Bars*. Low prices. Fast service. Fantastically flavorful food. (Try the goyza dumplings and the #43 noodles!) When I was a starving student, I went here at least once a week. www.wagamama.com

- *The Churchill Arms*. Kensington Church Street, London W8. Wacky atmosphere and extremely affordable. (Try the pad Thai and red duck curry.) Book ahead!

Still, sometimes a girl needs more than a restaurant and wants a *destination*. I hear you. If you want to mix with the cool, the hip, and the hungry, these are my picks for the perfect Girls Night Out:

- *Ping Pong*. Their motto is "Little steamed parcels of deliciousness," and they certainly deliver. Ping Pong has the best dim sum around, an extremely buzzy atmosphere, and hugely creative cocktails. Super-cheap and super-delicious! Locations all over London. www.pingpongdimsum.com

- *Eight Over Eight*. Asian tapas, sushi, and sashimi washed down with great cocktails. (Try the crispy crab salad and the

frozen berry dessert!) Closest tube: Sloane Square. www
.rickerrestaurants.com/

- *The Salt Yard.* Spanish tapas and wine to die for! Closest tube:
Goodge Street. www.saltyard.co.uk

- *Bam-Bou.* Mouthwatering French-Vietnamese food in a higgledy-piggledy Georgian town house. Make sure to have a
pre-dinner cocktail in the glamorous top-floor bar! Closest
tubes: Tottenham Court Road or Goodge Street. www.bam
-bou.co.uk

- *The Botanist.* This small, buzzing bar and restaurant right off
Sloane Square is literally overflowing with cute boys in tailored suits. An excellent place to wine and dine, while rubbing shoulders with the designer-clad Chelsea set. Thursday
nights are the best (and the most rambunctious). Closest
tube: Sloane Square. www.thebotanistonsloanesquare.com/

- *Anywhere in Lancashire Court.* This is one of London's hidden
gems. Not only do you feel like you're in a Dickens novel once
you step into this secret cobblestone mews, but the bars and
restaurants are always hopping and filled with flirtatious
Bright Young Things. Thursday and Friday nights are best.
Especially during nice weather. Closest tube: Bond Street.
www.lancashirecourt.com

## Phoning Home

Although London is still dotted with iconic red "phone boxes"—
they are becoming dangerously obsolete since everyone has a "mow-
bile." (Note that "mobile" should rhyme with *tile*—*not* with *noble*.)

The Carphone Warehouse is an oddly named UK chain that will help you compare and contrast the various phone companies available. Deals change all the time so every twelve months, check your options to see if you should switch providers. Some companies offer free calls to your top three US phone numbers. Others will give you a free 1-800 number that friends and family can use to call you in London if they don't have international dialing. Ask around and see what's out there. Don't forget to use your UK phone as little as humanly possible when back home in the US, as the roaming charges are extortionate.

Note: Getting a UK landline (and wireless broadband) connected in a new flat can take up to *six weeks*—so make sure you have alternative means for communication during this time.

# Exercise

If you live in London, you're likely to walk at least two to three miles a day—probably more. Want to burn off last night's Pinot Grigio? All you have to do is make sure you walk up the steps of the escalators rather than stand. This, combined with the UK's teeny portion sizes, means that it is much easier to stay fit in England than it is in the US (the land of cars and all-you-can-eat buffets).

Still, all those liquid calories can take their toll, and in an effort to counteract the damage, I shocked myself and joined a gym. I figured it would give me something do on the nights that I forbid myself to go out. (Many UK companies offer discounted rates to their employees, so take advantage of this if you can.)

However, a monthly gym membership can still be expensive, and it wasn't long before I had to acknowledge that structured exercise bored me senseless. Knowing I had to try something new, I ventured into a yoga studio. The first time I tried yoga, my arms were literally too weak for downward dog. But I persevered and to my surprise began to *like* it—a feeling toward physical activity I was certain never to possess. I like yoga because it is so much more than exercise—it's a philosophy, a way of life, it clears all that chatter in your mind, *and* it happens to involve amusing animal poses that help me not to be so bored.

My quest for affordable pay-as-you-go yoga classes led me to one of the best yoga centers in the world: The Life Centre is a sanctuary of tranquility—but they work you hard. After ninety minutes here I feel 90 percent more grounded than I did when I walked in. I can't recommend it enough. www.thelifecentre.com

Long to be as toned as royal sister-in-law Pippa Middleton? Her stunning figure has been a talking point since the royal wedding (the girl's bottom actually trended on Twitter), and now her fitness secret is out. Pippa goes to weekly pilates sessions at Pilates on the Go in Fulham's Parsons Green. You can even see her testimonial on their website. Make sure to request Margo Campbell as an instructor. www.pilatesonthego.co.uk

If you prefer to exercise outdoors, all London parks offer various fitness classes, which are a great way to get some fresh air and meet people in your area. And if you really want to multi-task getting fit with getting a guy, there are always Scottish dancing events happening somewhere. (See "More Regal Hunting Grounds," page 169). Still, I must reiterate that Chelsea Harbor Club is by far the best gym for meeting titled talent. www.harbourclubchelsea.com.

# Travel Home

I'll never forget the first time I had to fly home after spending my semester abroad in London. I was literally crying at Heathrow Airport, sobbing into the phone and begging my parents to let me stay in this land of my dreams just a little bit longer.

Yet things were different back then—flights weren't as cheap as they are now, and many Americans were taught to believe that once they went to Europe, they would most likely never be back again, so best to see as much as you possibly could while you were there. But things have changed. Cheap flights occasionally *can* be found, and as the world gets smaller and smaller, we'll find ourselves zigzagging across the oceans more and more.

Still, nothing is worse than trying to book your flight home and trawling through hundreds of travel sites trying to find something vaguely affordable—it makes me dizzy, and the longer I spend looking, the more expensive the flights become! But then I found Trailfinders, a travel agency that always manages to find the cheapest US flight available even if you're going to a tiny American town no one has ever heard of (www.trailfinders.com). One phone call—and you're done.

Don't forget to join the frequent flier program of each airline you ever take—if you live in the UK long enough, one day all those extra miles will come in handy.

# Dilemmas of Downsizing

*A man with one watch knows what time it is;*
*a man with two watches is never quite sure.*
—LEE SEGALL

One thing that living in London teaches you is that Americans have way, way too much. They have too many cars, too many rooms in their houses, and too many things in each room. Because England is such a minuscule country and it contains so many people, you quickly learn to downsize your life into a smaller space. In the beginning it's annoying and all you can do is grumble about how much space you used to have, but eventually the minimalist lifestyle begins to grow on you. And the upside of having no car and less space is that your spending is automatically curtailed.

## The Fridge/Freezer Dilemma

So your fridge is the size of a small television and you probably share it with three other people. The good news? When you go grocery shopping (Waitrose is best in terms of quality, price, and ethical standards), you literally can only buy what fits on your designated refrigerator shelf. Because you didn't drive to the grocery store, you literally can only buy items that you are physically strong enough to carry home with you. In reality, it was the latter that restrained my shopping more than anything. I'm not exactly Hercules, so lightweight food (asparagus, raspberries, dark chocolate) always took priority over heavier things like ice cream and potatoes. I may have been dying for a piece of cheesecake or chicken pot pie—but I knew I didn't have the storage space to bring a family size home with me (nor did I have the strength to carry one!). No freezer (warning: most UK flats have no freezer!) to store things meant I could only buy fresh food—which forced me to plan my weekly menus carefully and pay close attention to expiration dates. So something as simple as a small kitchen appliance forced me not to overbuy, overeat, and overspend—and in that way, it taught me not to be wasteful—something all those American shoppers with gigantic refrigerators probably will never learn in their lifetime.

## The Washing Machine/Dryer Dilemma

So your washing machine is so tiny you sometimes wonder if you'd be better off washing your clothes in a mixing bowl? Not to mention that there is no dryer to speak of and you are expected to hang all of your wet clothing on hot radiators (that fill the already damp house with steam) or on pioneer-style drying racks? I promise you it's not as depressing as it sounds—once you get used to it. As much as I love US washing facilities (mainly because they're so large I can fit inside them), using that much energy and doing that much laundry (especially as a singleton) is simply not necessary (or environmentally viable). Back in college I was the type of girl who would occasionally buy more underwear* to avoid doing laundry— but let's not talk about that since this is supposed to be about ideas for saving. But living in the UK taught me to embrace hand washing in a way that would make my grandmother proud. You don't have to scrub your clothes against a washboard or anything grueling like that; all you have to do is fill the sink with water, pop in a capful of delicate detergent, and throw in your items. Let them soak while you are in the shower and then rinse them clean. Now that I say it, it really is like doing your laundry in a sink-shaped mixing bowl—but much safer since UK washing machines usually turn your clothes gray. (Also, beware of machines that claim to be

* Just in case you're wondering, Marks & Spencer is the best place for cute and affordable "knickers."

washers *and* dryers into one—they neither clean nor dry.) I only risk my gym clothes, sheets, and pajamas in that weird UK appliance—everything else is hand-washed or, occasionally, dry-cleaned.

You'll find that because there are no dryers and clothes don't come out soft and wrinkle-free, the Brits are *obsessed* with ironing. They all iron their sheets (and will gasp in *horror* if you admit that you don't iron yours)—and I have personally witnessed several flatmates iron their jeans and underwear. I'm sorry, but that's where I draw the line. Luckily, cashmere and tweed don't require ironing.

# A Girl's Flat Is Her Castle

*Some people think luxury is the opposite of poverty.*
*It is not. It is the opposite of vulgarity.*
—Coco Chanel

A few months after I arrived in London, polo invitations weren't exactly pouring into my hands as I'd hoped. I had no social life, my money was dwindling at a terrifying speed, and I honestly felt that I had nothing to do but sit in my dark London bedroom, repaint my toenails, recalculate my debt, and die of frustration.

And the craziest part was that I was absolutely miserable in the place I was certain would make me the happiest.

Still, if you know me at all—you'll know that I am not easily daunted. After a few days of feeling sorry for myself, I'd had enough. When it comes to your surroundings, sometimes the smallest luxuries are all it takes to make a girl feel more like a princess than a pauper. Many of these are what I like to call "palace essentials"—

which basically means you need to ask yourself what Queen Elizabeth I would insist upon to brighten the dreary rooms of her palaces. So here are seven small . . .

WAYS TO MAKE YOUR LIFE MORE REGAL:

- Fresh flowers. It sounds crazy, but I truly believe that in the fast-moving chaos of London life, stopping to observe the beauty of a fresh flower can help connect us (however briefly) to the noble beauty in ourselves.* So I went to Urban Outfitters, bought a simple glass bud vase, and every *fortnight* (that's Brit talk for "two weeks") thereafter, I'd purchase a single white rose or a small bunch of alstroemeria—both of which have a long-lasting vase life of up to fourteen days. (Avoid tulips—they may be inexpensive but they wilt quickly. And never have artificial flowers—they get dusty, usually look cheap, and, according to the principles of feng shui—symbolize lifelessness.)

- Good coffee. Forget buying coffee in London; finding rich, American-style java (much less unlimited refills) is simply impossible and there is no point paying a fortune (up to $9 a cup!) for espresso at any of the various chains. If I gave up my coffee for a year, I'd probably be able to cover a month's rent—but I'd be far too grumpy to care! So I did what any girl would do—I bought a cheap French coffee press and then went to Wedgwood to purchase a single china coffee cup. Using grounds brought over in my suitcase from the US, I

---

* Buddha is said to have given a silent sermon during which he simply held up a flower and gazed at it.

made my own coffee every morning. I may not have known what the rest of my London day was going to be like, but at least I could guarantee that for those few perfect sips, the world was as it should be. (I realize that Queen Elizabeth I technically drank a mug of ale in the morning, but the sentiment still applies. So stay with me.)

- Velvet cushions. One or two is all it takes to make a dull room feel more sumptuous. John Lewis has a great selection of plush jewel tones—I even managed to find one emblazoned with a royal crest.

- A good candle. Choose something slow-burning, with a regal aroma (Diptyque is my favorite).

- Music from the Tudor Courts. *Historic Royal Palaces* has a huge range. I listen to "Crowns & Coronations" or "Henry VIII: Heads & Hearts" (don't laugh) at least once a week—I can always count on theses ethereal CDs to soothe me back to my natural state of royal calm. www.historicroyalpalaces .com/cds-and-dvds/cd-s.html

- Quality perfume. Queen Elizabeth I liked rose and lavender water, but I prefer Chanel.

- Quality chocolate. (At least 60 percent cocoa solids.)* Elizabethan England used chocolate purely for medicinal purposes, and I think it's fair for you to do the same.

---

* Most American "chocolate" cannot legally be called chocolate in Europe since the cocoa content falls below their strict legal standards.

# Converting

Converting British sterling to American dollars is never a pleasant experience. It only works in your favor if you're earning pounds and spending dollars—not vice versa. But if you're earning dollars and spending pounds, it's best if you know the most up-to-date exchange rate. So bookmark the following on your computer or buy the app. Oanda is the most accurate converter I've found so far and the most user-friendly. www.oanda.com/currency/converter

# British Banks

*Feel the thrill of totting up a balanced book*
*A thousand ciphers neatly in a row!*
*When gazing at a graph that shows the profits up*
*Your little cup of joy should overflow*
—MARY POPPINS

Oftentimes a UK university or UK employer will set up a British bank account for you. But in some cases you'll have to do it yourself. As part of the UK's money laundering legislation, British banks must establish your identity when you open an account. It can't hurt to bring a reference from your US bank, but by law the British bank will need to see one identification document (like a passport) and one address verification document (something formally addressed to you at your UK address).

This is a bit of a catch-22 as it's quite hard to establish a UK address unless you have money to pay the rent. That said, until you set up your UK bank account, make sure your US bank account offers the following:

- no ATM fees when you withdraw cash abroad

- a credit or debit card without fees for overseas purchases

- online banking

- a twenty-four-hour helpline

- the ability to quickly transfer money internationally (For this you will need to know routing numbers, SWIFT codes, and BIC numbers.)

As you'd expect, British banks offer a staggering array of accounts to choose from. As part of preparing for your move to London, go to MoneySupermarket to compare what's on offer in terms of interest rates, etc (www.moneysupermarket.com/current -accounts).

KNOW THE BANKING LINGO:

- *current account:* a checking account.

- *standing order:* These are regular bank transfers to a company or person. You may need to organize one of these for your rent. Ask your landlord for a standing order form, fill it in, and give the completed form to your bank.

- *direct debit:* This is similar to a standing order, but instead of returning the completed form to the bank, you return the form to a company that you authorize to take money from your account. Most Brits use direct debits to pay for regular household bills.

- *chip and pin:* In the UK (and across Europe), they don't rely on signatures to authorize card payments. Instead, your debit and credit cards are fitted with a microchip and private pin number—which is much more secure. (The downside is that you have one more thing to memorize.)

- *cheques* (that's the UK spelling of "checks"): These aren't used in the UK as much as they are in the US. Debit cards that take money directly from your checking account are preferred, and most bills are paid online via bank transfers or direct debits (although you can still send a cheque, if you prefer).

- *overdraft*: Imagine my surprise when I learned that bouncing cheques in the UK is entirely allowed! Don't get excited—they do charge you for the privilege and you need to have something called an "agreed overdraft." An overdraft allows you to take money out of your checking account even when the balance is zero. You can only take up to an agreed limit (usually £500) and interest is payable on the amount you take. (If you are a student, you may be offered an interest-free overdraft.) Still, this handy facility definitely helps you get by from pay cheque to pay cheque and is a lot cheaper than borrowing money on a credit card.

TAXES:

- Most UK employers automatically deduct all UK tax from your salary; this is called "Pay As You Earn" (or PAYE) and is great because it means no paperwork and no saving for a big tax bill at the end of the year.

- You only need to file a separate UK tax return if you are self-employed.

- The good news is that the UK tax return is a bazillion times easier to fill out than the US version, so hiring an expensive London accountant is usually not necessary.

- Don't forget that US citizens are still obligated to file a US tax return once a year during the time they are overseas (which means you might have to file two tax returns per year).

- In most cases you'll pay so much tax in the UK that you are not required to pay any tax in the US (but you still have to fill out the form explaining this to the US government).

## Staying Focused

*We are all in the gutter, but some of us are looking at the stars.*
—Oscar Wilde

Growing up in the heartland of America, everyone around me scoffed at my big London dreams. But I ignored them. I truly believed that if I continued to define the life that I wanted, continued to focus on it with all of my intention—and was ready to claim it with all of my heart—eventually the universe would provide it for me.

Even back then, I somehow sensed that I needed to visualize my intentions if I wanted them to materialize. So I plastered my bedroom walls with dozens of glossy posters: black-and-white photographs of London's famous landmarks; pictures of London's sparkling night skylines; beautiful prints of Buckingham Palace, Kensington Palace, Hampton Court Palace, and the Crown Jewels.

Late at night, when I became infuriated with my high school chemistry equations, my tired eyes would always wander away from my desk and settle onto my wonderful English posters. Sometimes it seemed that if I stared at those posters hard enough, I could somehow transport myself into them.

And in a way, I have done just that! Gone are the days of small town America! (I now *live* in *London*!) Gone are the days of life on a shoestring! (I now get *paid* to write about *England*!) Gone are the days of sorrowful singlehood! (I recently married a handsome *Englishman* at Hampton Court Palace!) My enchanted life is of course a mixture of luck and dogged determination—but I owe a lot of it to the law of attraction. You are the designer of your own destiny, and I truly believe that what you think about, you bring about. And for this reason, I implore you to create *a vision board*.

A vision board is nothing more than a visual collage of your dreams that helps you to manifest them into reality. The law of attraction states that we attract the things that we give the most attention to. For example, if you repeat the words "yellow, yellow, yellow" and you start looking around you, all the yellow things will automatically stand out. In exactly the same way, if you repeat your dreams to yourself over and over, you will be shocked to discover the ways in which they start coming true.

HOW TO CREATE A VISION BOARD:

- Define the life you want. Ask yourself exactly where you want to be, exactly what you want to do, exactly where you want to live and with whom.

- Find pictures of these dreams in old magazines or search for them on Google images. Don't be embarrassed if your chosen photos contain nothing but castles, jewels, polo ponies, and princes. All that matters is that each picture you choose evokes an emotional response within you and represents something that you genuinely desire.

🞂 Find inspiring quotes to help feed messages of purpose and conviction into your subconscious and add these to the mix.

🞂 Paste your photos and inspirational words onto a piece of paper and put it up someplace where you will see it every single day. The mere sight of your vision board should make you happy. Every time you look at it, let it fuel your passion to go after your dreams.

Continue to focus your thoughts on the life that you know you are destined for—and don't be surprised when you wake up one day and find yourself living it.

## Counting Your Money (and Your Blessings)

*You have cause for nothing but gratitude and joy.*
—Buddha

If you're anything like me, finance is not your forte and adding extra currencies to the mix hardly helps matters. This is precisely why girls like us must rigorously keep track of and count our money. But it's equally important that we keep track of and count our *blessings*. It's impossible to bring abundance into your London life if you are not grateful for the fact that you are already in London! If you are actively thankful for the blessings you already possess, and remind yourself daily of all you are grateful for, you are actually summoning even more abundance to you. This is why I keep a gratitude journal, and so should you.

1. Grab a notebook—or invest in something prettier with a soft leather cover.

2. Every morning, jot down five things that you are thankful for—your family, your friends, your health, the boy in your life, the city that you live in, the day-to-day joys that occur just because you're in England . . .

3. Don't worry about your handwriting—just get them down on the page, and as you do so feel the gratitude in your heart. The gratitude should be so intense and so genuine that you can feel tears coming to your eyes because for those few moments, you remember precisely how much these things mean to you.

4. Next, be grateful for the things that *are coming your way*: a UK work permit, your dream job, your dream man . . . Be specific and be detailed. List the things you are thankful for *in the present tense*. Whether you have them yet or not is irrelevant—the gratitude you feel for the fact that you *will have them* should be just as real as it is for the things you already have.

5. Notice how your mood changes almost immediately. If you start your day by reminding yourself of your blessings, you are naturally empowered to deal with any obstacles (financial or otherwise) that you might encounter before bedtime.

RECOMMENDED READING:

*Confessions of a Shopaholic* by **Sophie Kinsella**

I'm sure you've probably read it already, but if you haven't, you need to—not the movie, not the spin-off books, but the original novel that started it all. When I first read this book, I was convinced that it was based on my life—a girl living in a trendy SW flat, drowning in debt, chasing after cute British clothes and even cuter British boys? (Come on, clearly I inspired the plot in *some* way.) I love this book because our fair heroine, Becky Bloomwood, eventually shows us that living within our means does not ruin our chances of living happily ever after. What can I say? Sometimes classic chick lit is downright inspiring.


RECOMMENDED VIEWING:

*The Secret* DVD by **Rhoda Byrne**

The entire idea of *The Secret* has caused quite a stir recently, yet when I first heard about it, I thought, "But that's exactly what I've always done!" Basically, *The Secret* features a series of authors, philosophers, doctors, quantum physicists, and entrepreneurs expounding on the power of positive thinking and how it can be applied to defining and claiming the life you were destined for. Like mind over matter, *The Secret* shows us how mind over *money* begins with believing you deserve it and knowing that it will come.

# NINE

# EXPAT ESSENTIALS

*When it's three o'clock in New York,*
*it's still 1938 in London.*
—BETTE MIDLER

## Parable #7

The place is London. The date is the day before Thanksgiving. I was grocery shopping in Waitrose when I spotted a blond woman doubled over in tears in the baking aisle. I could tell by the way she was perfectly groomed that she was probably American (but even if that didn't give it away, I could see a giant turkey in her shopping trolley).

I asked if she was okay.

"I can't find *marshmallows!*" she sobbed. "How am I supposed to make yams without marshmallows? I've looked *everywhere* . . . How hard can it be to find marshmallows? I *hate* this country!"

As she continued hiccupping hopelessly, I gently suggested that she try Partridges, a gourmet food store on King's Road that specializes in American products. She looked at me like I had just offered to give her a million dollars.

I'm glad I was able to help.

For those times when you simply can't go another day without Ritz crackers, Pop-Tarts, and Apple Jacks, here are three places that stock those essential (almost always fattening) foodstuffs that make us proud to be American:

- *Partridges.* It's expensive here (think $9 for Stove Top Stuffing)—but I have been known to indulge my craving for Instant Quaker Oatmeal (Maple Brown Sugar flavor) on more than one occasion. www.partridges.co.uk

- *Whole Foods.* I think the American expat community breathed a collective sigh of relief when Whole Foods opened its flagship European store on High Street Kensington. Finally a place that understands our needs! The shop is three stories high, is the location of London's first ever food court, and is staffed almost entirely by friendly Americans. They even offer "Thanksgiving consultants" to help our frazzled countrymen in their time of need. They are also very expensive, but they bake a mean corn bread and actually know what you're talking about when you ask for corn syrup or cranberry sauce. www.wholefoodsmarket.com/stores/kensington

- *Sky Co.* A great online service that delivers your favorite American groceries to your door. Thanks to them, you never have to wait too long when your stomach starts yearning for Goldfish crackers. www.skyco.uk.com

# Parable #8

The setting is London. The date is the day before Halloween. I find myself breaking into tears in the middle of the street. I have been to five stores, including Whole Foods. I have called countless on-line vendors. But no matter what I try, it seems hopeless. *I can't find dry ice!* And my Halloween party is *tomorrow*!

Oh, how smug I was when I comforted that poor American woman about her marshmallows. But there I was at my wit's end—just like her! Why is dry ice so hard to find? For god's sake, they hand it out for free at every grocery store in America! My English husband didn't understand my frustration—mainly because he'd never seen dry ice before and had no idea how magical it could be and how essential it was for an authentic Halloween party.

Finally, I called an industrial ice supplier.

"We can give you some for eighty pounds," the woman on the phone told me. "And that's assuming you understand that dry ice is not for domestic use."*

"Um, of course," I lied. "But exactly how much ice would eighty pounds get me?"

"A piece about the size of a brick."

Right. Rather than pay $150 for a large ice cube that she'd already told me I couldn't legally use, I hung up and called another industrial ice supplier. (Can you tell I was desperate to throw the perfect party?)

"Listen," the guy tells me, "if you come to our Heathrow

---

* Apparently hydrogen peroxide is not meant for domestic use in the UK either!

warehouse around 7 a.m. tomorrow—I'll give you some on the sly. But you can't tell anyone."

So my husband and I got up early and drove nearly ten miles outside of town to make a back-alley dry-ice pickup. And I'm so glad we did.

I put dry ice in dozens of mini cauldrons around our flat and the Brits went *wild*. They'd never seen anything like it in their lives. Those drunk, costumed Englishmen were like giddy schoolboys in a mad scientist lab—pouring dry ice into their drinks, into the bathtub, into their beer . . . by the end of the night, someone had dumped the entire cooler of contraband ice into the shower and turned it on full blast. Years later, English friends still refer to that party as "Gorillas in the Mist."

The lesson? American-themed parties make you stand out as a hostess. (They also allow you to fulfill any homesickness you might be feeling around these US holidays.) So every year I make sure to throw a 4th of July party (the Brits go berserk when I serve key lime pie), a Halloween party, and a Thanksgiving dinner. I even do an occasional Groundhog Day cocktail party—which is hugely popular, especially when I project live broadcasts of Punxsutawney Phil's prognostications.

Long ago I learned that it's okay not to be English. What's not okay is being ashamed that you're not English. So embrace those nutty American traditions, make an effort to be authentic, and show those stuffy Brits that when it comes to holidays, no one does it better. (Just try not to get thrown in jail for using dry ice.)

# Making English Friends

*Never refuse an invitation, never resist the unfamiliar,*
*never fail to be polite and never outstay the welcome.*
—Leonardo DiCaprio

During my first summer in England, I read a fantastic new novel*
set in London—the themes of which were keeping me permanently
distracted. Aside from a rather elaborate murder plot, the book was
about an American girl who'd regularly head to Hyde Park at sun-
rise to watch the early morning joggers go by. Of course, it wasn't
long before she caught the eye of a dashing upper-class English boy
who happened to be running past her—and soon the two of them
were madly in love. Aside from the getting up at dawn part, I was
hoping to see if this approach might work for me.

But no such luck.

I'd patiently sit on *my* park bench for hours upon hours—
watching people jog around the duck pond or row along the Ser-
pentine; watching children with their adorable school uniforms
clamber around on the Princess Diana Memorial Playground. I
knew some of these humans had to be English, but it was as if an
invisible glass wall existed between us—keeping our worlds di-
vided. And soon I came to realize that meeting people in England
simply by "catching their eye" was pure and utter fiction.

Like it or not, in England you don't strike up casual conversation with strangers. You just don't. You could sit next to the
same person on the same train for twenty-five years, and you still

---

* *The Drowning People*, written by nineteen-year-old, floppy-haired Old Eto-
nian Richard Mason.

wouldn't dare speak to them. Anyone who breaks this inherent English rule is deemed dangerous at best.

In large American cities, everyone comes and goes so quickly that there is a general openness to new blood and new friendships. But in London, everyone is already firmly and happily ensconced in their college social circle, so there is very little incentive for them to make new friends.

And unlike Americans, who will happily introduce themselves to anyone who makes eye contact (and even to those who don't), Brits wait to be formally introduced. As I mentioned before, there is actually an embarrassment in certain English circles of introducing anyone to anyone, because of course everyone is supposed to know everyone already. If they don't know someone or that someone's family—it means that long ago (sometimes even centuries ago) that family was deemed not worth knowing. The whole American idea of "networking" is looked down upon with contempt because to the Brits it implies a certain degree of social climbing. Anyone attempting to mix outside of their circle must be suspect or they wouldn't have to attempt it in the first place.

I'd lived in London quite a while before I began to comprehend this antiquated British thinking. When I was doing my master's degree, I remember asking the registrar if there was any kind of student directory so I could find out who was in my class and keep in touch with them. The British university administrator looked at me like I was absolutely crazy.

"That information is *confidential*," she told me snootily.

Circa 2002, all my American friends were on MySpace and Friendster, yet when I extended electronic invites to my London friends, every single one of them refused. They just didn't get the idea of connecting with people—even people they knew! But ever so slowly the landscape changed and a small tipping point was achieved. Before I knew what was happening, English friends were inviting *me* to join this cool new thing called Facebook. (I have to admit that my very first Facebook invite came from my now sister-in-law—who is English.)

But the initial reason the Brits liked Facebook so much was because they viewed it as something socially exclusive—another fun way to let some people in and keep others out—the very definition of their beloved class system. (There is a joke that says if you place three Englishmen in a room, they will create an exclusive club for two.) But the good news is that technology and, dare I say it, the rise of the meritocracy is breaking down these barriers. And what do you know—suddenly the English are networking with the rest of us, which means more than ever before, they are willing to befriend an American. (They just won't share their life story within minutes of making your acquaintance.)

IDEAS FOR MAKING BRITISH FRIENDS:

1. Get a job. If you can't get a job, get an unpaid internship. Start volunteering. Just do something that will take you away from other Americans and allow you to mix with real British people.

2. Live with British people. (See Chapter 1.)

3. Throw a cocktail party and invite your office mates—the rule being that they must invite at least one other person that no one else knows. You'll find that the Brits are secretly very curious about American holiday traditions, so the more American the party—the larger the turnout will be. (See Parable #8.) If you can't squeeze everyone into your flat, organize an evening picnic in a local park. In bad weather, congregate at a

local pub or book the upstairs bar at the Texas Embassy—it's free and it's one of the best American bar spaces in the city. www.texasembassy.com

4. Organize a neighborhood get-together. Brits are so socially reserved that they usually don't know any of their neighbors, even if they want to. So take the lead. Print out some invites and slide them under all the doors in your building or into all the mailboxes on your street. When I lived in Maida Vale, I organized a singles party this way, stating "You don't have to be single, as long as you bring someone who is." My British flatmates were certain no one would show up. In the end, our garden was filled with nearly fifty people—the party went on far into the night and spilled into all the adjoining flats on our hall. The Brits *want* to meet people—they just don't know how!

5. Get a dog. I know it's a lifetime commitment, but the minute I had a pooch with me, suddenly England seemed like America—strangers were absolutely clamoring to talk to me, and now I know at least twenty people in my neighborhood. London has one of the largest and most innovative puppy rescue centers in the world. Check it out (also good for volunteering): Battersea Dogs and Cats Home, www.battersea .org.uk. (Queen Victoria was their first ever patron.)

6. Go Scottish dancing. I realize this is like the third time I've mentioned this, but I'm telling you—the benefits abound. (See "More Regal Hunting Grounds," page 169.)

7. Start a book club. Everyone wants to join a book club, but no one ever gets around to starting one. This is where you come

in. Choose a book that you love (best to start with something you know to be good rather than dragging readers through something awful), invite a handful of people, and again, tell them to invite one other person no one else knows. Hold your first meeting at a fun venue like the Lanesborough Hotel's Library Bar, www.lanesborough.com/#culinary_experience/library_bar, or the Book Club Bar, www.wearetbc.com.

After the first meeting, take turns choosing books and venues. Don't beat yourselves up if you stop talking about the book after five minutes and drink wine for the rest of the night. (FYI: another fun literary night out is Book Slam, www.bookslam.com.)

8. Join the Fulham Women's Institute (WI). Founded in 1915, the Women's Institute is kind of like the UK equivalent of the Junior League. Traditionally, the WI attracted a much older crowd, until a few years ago, when a group of London twenty-somethings in the SW area decided to create "a modern women's group with a traditional ethos." They throw great balls and do excellent charity work—you can't go wrong. www.fulhamwi.org.uk

## Expat Groups

There are quite a few American women's groups in London. While it can be tempting to reach out to these groups right away, keep in mind that it may not help your immersion into English life, as many members end up socializing only with other Americans. If you do decide to join one, make sure you do at least one thing from the list above as well.

- Kensington & Chelsea Women's Club (This one tends to be more international than the others and manages to secure some amazing speakers—Lady Sarah Bradford, John Simpson, and Yours Truly to name just a few.) www.kcwc.org.uk

- St. John's Wood Women's Club, www.sjwwc.org.uk

- Hampstead Women's Club, hwcinlondon.co.uk/Home

- Surrey American Women's Club, www.awsurrey.org

- American Women's Club of London, www.awclondon.org

- The London Ladies Club, www.londonladies.co.uk

- Also, get in touch with your sorority back at home and ask if there is an alumni chapter in London—most of them have one, and it's always fun to reconnect with girls with whom you have something in common other than nationality.

## A Country of Countries

Please note that the United Kingdom, Great Britain, and England are all different places, and Americans are secretly laughed at if they use the terms incorrectly, so pay close attention to the following:

- **The United Kingdom of Great Britain and Northern Ireland:** The UK is a "country of countries," made up of four coequal sovereign countries: England, Wales, Scotland, and Northern Ireland. You can call them all "British" (as their inhabitants all have British passports and are considered British citizens), but the four countries generally don't like one another, so to avoid offense, try to be specific and use the terms "English," "Welsh," "Scottish," and "Northern Irish" when referring to a person's national identity.

- **Great Britain:** A geographical rather than a political term, "Great Britain" refers to the largest island among the British Isles and contains England, Wales, and Scotland.

- **England:** The largest and most populated country in the UK, containing its capital city, London.

- **Ireland:** Again this is a geographical rather than a political term. The island of Ireland contains two countries: Northern Ireland and the Republic of Ireland. Note that people from the Republic of Ireland are Irish (*not* Northern Irish).

- **European Union:** Both the UK and the Republic of Ireland are members of the European Union, but the UK does not use the Euro as its currency.

## The Sun Never Sets . . .

As you know, the Queen's face appears on money all over the world. Indeed, at the peak of its power, it was often said that "the sun never sets on the British Empire" because its span across the globe ensured that the sun was always shining on at least one of its numerous territories. Read on to understand the difference between the Empire and the Commonwealth and how the UK fits into it all.

- The *British Empire* consists of the dominions, colonies, protectorates, mandates, and other territories ruled or administered by the United Kingdom. By 1922, the British Empire held sway over nearly *one-quarter of the world's population* and covered almost a *quarter of the Earth's total land area*! However, after World War II, many countries sought their independence from the British Empire, and over the next twenty years, British rule ended in many parts of Africa, Asia, the Caribbean, the Mediterranean, and the Pacific.

- The *Commonwealth* (warning: this is where it gets complicated) is a voluntary association of fifty-three independent countries, many of which were former British colonies. Most countries gained their independence from the Empire through diplomacy and opted to join the Commonwealth. Commonwealth countries can have different constitutions: a republic with a president as head of state (such as India and South Africa), an indigenous monarchy (such as Lesotho and Tonga), a sultanate (Brunei), or a realm recognizing the Queen as sovereign (such as Canada and Australia). Whichever form their constitution takes, all member countries recognize Her Majesty Queen Elizabeth II as Head of the Commonwealth.

- A *Commonwealth Realm* is a country that has HM Queen Elizabeth II as its monarch and head of state. There are fifteen Commonwealth realms in addition to the UK: Australia, New Zealand, Canada, Jamaica, Antigua and Barbuda, Belize, Papua New Guinea, St. Christopher and Nevis, St. Vincent and the Grenadines, Tuvalu, Barbados, Grenada, the Solomon Islands, St. Lucia, and the Bahamas.

- *British Overseas Territories (formerly known as Crown Colonies)* are the fourteen territories outside the British Isles over which Britain retains legal sovereignty. These include: Anguilla, Bermuda, the British Antarctic Territory, the British Indian Ocean Territory (BIOT), the British Virgin Islands (BVI), the Cayman Islands, the Sovereign Base Areas of Akrotiri and Dhekelia on Cyprus, the Falkland Islands, Gibraltar, Montserrat, the Pitcairn Islands, St. Helena and its dependencies (Ascension Island and Tristan da Cunha), South Georgia and the South Sandwich Islands, and the Turks and Caicos Islands.

- The *Crown Dependencies* are the Isle of Man and the Channel Islands (Baliwick of Jersey and Baliwick of Guernsey). They are technically not part of the United Kingdom but are still dependent territories of the English Crown. This means that although they have their own administration, the UK government still handles certain areas of policy.

## Gin and Tonic: A Very Brief History

When the British were busy colonizing India and other exotic regions of their far-flung Empire, they began drinking tonic water (which contains quinine) in order to ward off malaria. Of course it wasn't long before the Brits, being Brits, decided to add gin. Hence, one of the best drinks on earth was born.

# Eating in England

*English cuisine is generally so threadbare that for years there
has been a gentlemen's agreement in the civilized world to
allow the Brits preeminence in the matter of tea—which, after
all, comes down to little more than the ability to boil water.*
—WILIFRED SHEED

"How do you *cope* in England?" American friends ask me, "Aren't
you *starving*? What do you *eat* over there? Don't they put mayonnaise on *everything*?"

I will admit that it is easier to find good food in America than it
is the UK. In America you can pretty much walk into any hole-in-
the-wall and expect a certain level of quality, much less edibility.
You'll also probably find that American waiters take a genuine interest in, and will happily discuss with you, whether you'd most
enjoy your steak with béarnaise sauce or peppercorn gravy.

Not so in the UK. You can't just randomly walk into any cafe
or restaurant or pub and expect the food or service to be good. Because it won't be.

Please keep in mind that it was little more than twenty years ago
that the Brits discovered avocados, much less olive oil. Which kind
of explains why many of them still enjoy overcooked meat, overcooked root vegetables, and lots of potatoes, washed down with lots
of alcohol. And because the service industry is based on salaries
rather than tips, customer service is not exactly stellar.

Nevertheless, London has come a long way in the last ten years.
Whereas before you were lucky if you could find decent tea and
toast, suddenly the capital is teeming with designer coffee shops,
trendy sushi bars, French bakeries, organic butchers, and cuisine
from every corner of the globe.

Will you be able to find pancakes and waffles? Probably not. But you will be able to taste some of the best Indian, Chinese, and Thai food in the world. Will you be able to find an authentic Caesar salad or New York bagel? Never. But you'll soon find yourself yearning for bangers and mash,* shepherd's pie, and sticky toffee pudding.

Still, when it comes to eating in England, I feel it is my duty to warn you about certain things so you are not shocked when you first encounter them:

- "Chips" means French fries not potato chips—which are known as "crisps."

- The UK boasts some of the most disturbing crisp flavors on earth (Prawn Cocktail, Chili & Squid, Lamb & Mint, Ham & Cranberry, Cheddar & Beer, to name just a few).

- Baked potatoes are known as "jacket potatoes." But don't expect sour cream and chives. The Brits prefer toppings such as canned corn, baked beans, tuna fish, and mayonnaise. I wish I were joking. (I have actually found a product that offers corn, beans, tuna, and mayonnaise all mixed together in the same can. I mailed one to my friend in New York and it scared her out of her wits.) They also like to put these very same toppings on pizza. Again, I wish were joking.

- Brits like to pour heavy cream on everything—including cheesecake.

---

* A *banger* is a sausage (much fatter and with more seasoning than breakfast sausages in the US). Bangers are usually served with mashed potatoes (*mash*) and onion gravy—if the meat is good quality, this is one of the best comfort foods in existence.

ᶾ⃕ Brits never "go out for ice cream" like Americans do. In fact the only time ice cream seems to be consumed is at the movie theater (aka the "cinema"). This is just as well because cinema popcorn is stale and cold—never hot, never freshly popped, and never drizzled with butter.

ᶾ⃕ A "full English breakfast" is famously considered among the natives to be the best cure for a hangover. This traditionally consists of fried toast, fried bacon, fried sausages, fried tomatoes, fried mushrooms, and fried eggs sunny-side-up—all served with a giant side of baked beans smothered in something called brown sauce. (But if you ask me, it should also be considered the best guaranteed route to a heart attack.)

ᶾ⃕ When Brits wash their dishes in the sink (aka when they do the "washing up"), they don't rinse them. I have no idea why this is and I have had countless debates with them on the subject—but they adamantly *insist* that rinsing off dish soap is entirely unnecessary. (Luckily, restaurants are required to use hygienically sound industrial dishwashers.)

## Places to AVOID
## (You might want to print this list out and keep it with you)

> *The only thing I know is that a real Londoner, a real one,*
> *would never, ever, ever eat at one of those bloody Angus*
> *bloody Steak Houses in the West End.*
> —FROM *LONDONERS*, BY CRAIG TAYLOR

London is full of tourist traps designed to appeal to Americans—they are branded in a cheerful way that Americans respond to and recognize, but the food is horrendous. *Please* trust me on this and don't be lured into any of the following:

- Aberdeen Steak House

- Angus Steak House

- Bella Italia

- Cafe Rouge

- Café Uno

- Chez Gerrard

- Garfunkel's

- La Tasca

- Millie's cookies (Ben's is so much better!)

- Pizza Hut & KFC (They're *not* like the ones in the US!)

However, there are several London chains all over the city offering coffee, pastries, salads, sandwiches, and even sushi—perfect for grabbing a quick bite for breakfast or lunch. All are affordable and of good quality:

- Apostrophe

- Café Nero

- Coffee Republic

- Costa Coffee

- Crush

- EAT

- Gail's (For the best blueberry muffins and chocolate chip cookies in the city.)

- Hummingbird Bakery

- Itsu Sushi

- LEON

- M&S Food

- Pan Quotidian

- Paul

- Prêt A Manger

- Ottolenghi (More expensive than the others but worth every penny. When the Barefoot Contessa came to London, this was her first stop.)

## More Favorites:

BEST VEGETARIAN RESTAURANT

- *The Gate.* Even die-hard carnivores love this place! www .thegate.tv

BEST FISH AND CHIPS

- *Geales.* www.geales.com

BEST "CURRY" (INDIAN FOOD)

> ✦ *Tandoori Lane.* 131 Munster Road, SW6. (Try the chicken specials and king prawn madras!) Closest tube: Parsons Green

## Craving Mexican Food?

I don't blame you. England is just getting to grips with Mexican food, and you'll find that more often than not they try to Europeanize it by adding ingredients like shredded duck meat and goat cheese. Still, two great restaurants have appeared lately that, while not entirely authentic, are as close as you're going to get:

> ✦ *Wahaca,* www.wahaca.co.uk

> ✦ *Crazy Homies,* www.crazyhomies.com/menu.html

## Craving Surf 'n' Turf or Pecan Pie?

Sometimes a girl needs a taste of home. There are lots of restaurants in London that call themselves "American," but most are anything but. Thank god for the Big Easy. It is the one place in London that genuinely feels like a little slice of the USA. The food portions are large and the cooking is entirely authentic. Live music on the weekends. www.bigeasy.co.uk

## Tipping

In London restaurants it is customary to tip approximately 10 percent, though it is more and more common to see a service charge already included on your bill, usually for 12.5 percent. Don't forget that unlike US servers, waiters and waitresses in the UK actually make minimum wage and aren't reliant on tips to supplement their income. This is why they are not especially nice to you.

## Splitting the Check

This is not a big deal in the UK, and I've regularly seen groups of twenty or more paying for their meal with twenty separate credit cards.

# Searching for a Skilled Salon . . . ?
# Aren't We All

## Puzzling Pedicures

For the longest time, I never understood why so many British women had such awful looking toenails. I mean how hard is it to clip them straight and brush on some polish? But on hot days in London, I'd be sitting on the steamy train and observing in horror row upon row of exposed feet bedecked in their best summer sandals. Peeking out of these sandals were unspeakable toenails—twice as long as anything you'd ever see in America and rather than cut straight across the top, they were *curved*, sometimes practically pointed! It was as if everyone was trying to reproduce long, painted fingernails on their feet! I was horrified, and baffled as to how and why British women thought this was appropriate. Until one day, I was browsing through Boots (a UK drugstore) and came across special toenail scissors that actually cut your nails in a curved shape. So that explained it. But it certainly didn't justify it.

As an American in London, I'm confident that you won't succumb to such savagery and purchase these scissors. But if you're hoping for an affordable, American-style pedicure, prepare to be disappointed. Don't expect comfy vibrating chairs with built-in Jacuzzi foot baths as a matter of course. Even many of the expensive spas provide nothing more than a normal chair and a plastic tub of warm water. One well-known spa (which shall remain nameless) didn't even bother to get my feet wet! So I've learned to take care of my toes myself. Believe me, even a self-pedicure will look better than 99 percent of the toes that are out there.

Still, if you must get your pedi fix, try these (they are at least *attempting* to emulate American standards):

- Julie Nails, Notting Hill Gate, W11
- The Nail Boutique, Sydney Street, SW3
- Hand and Foot Spa, Fulham Road, SW3

## Hair Hitches

Obtaining heavenly hair in the UK is difficult. After nearly fifteen years here, I have yet to walk out of a salon entirely happy—and I've been to every celebrity stylist on the block (including the royal coiffure of the moment, Richard Ward, who did Kate's hair on her wedding day). Yet I can walk into any no-name salon in small town America and emerge looking fabulous—perfect classic cut, sublimely bouncy dry. I just don't get it. Maybe it's because I have very thick, very curly hair and English stylists simply aren't used to handling such foreign textured tresses. Maybe it's because when I ask for a classic Jackie O or Grace Kelly shape, most stylists have no idea what I'm referring to. Maybe it's because London hairstylists are so über-trendy that they are simply incapable of creating anything other than an asymmetrical, rock-chick haircut. (And I'm telling you; even the *dogs* in New York City get better blow-dries.) Whatever the reason, I'm no longer taking risks with my best feature. English highlights are fine, but when it comes to cut and finish—it may be worth waiting for your next trip to America.* And considering how expensive some of these UK salons are, sometimes a flight from London to New York is actually *cheaper*. (Also see Chapter 9, "Fake It Till You Make It.")

# When Your Friends and Family Come to Visit

No matter how much you want to host them, usually your London flat will be so small that your friends and family will be forced to sleep on the floor, on the sofa, or even in your bed. Finding cheap accommodation in London that offers more than third world living conditions is not easy—but after years of research, these are my recommendations:

- *The Temple Lodge Club*. This B&B does not advertise, and I'd walked right by it for years before realizing it existed.

---

* If you know of a London salon that meets your American standards, please let me know! *info@jerramyfine.com*

Located adjacent to the best vegetarian restaurant in London, the Temple Lodge Club is a tiny oasis in the middle of Hammersmith. Housed in a gorgeous Georgian building, the rooms aren't exactly luxurious, but they are clean and they are cheap, and it's the best bargain you will find for such a central location. My bohemian father loves this place. www.templelodgeclub.com

- *High Road House.* This hotel is owned and operated by the fabulous Soho House group. You don't have to be a member to rent a room from this particular club, and because it's on the edge of West London (Turnham Green), the room rates are drastically cheaper that what you will find elsewhere. Still, you can reach central London in less than fifteen minutes by tube, so the location is actually extremely convenient for those who want to sightsee. Book early as these rooms get snapped up quickly! http://house.highroadhouse.co.uk

- *The Rockwell.* I suggested this hotel to my out-of-town wedding guests because it was the most affordable *and the most stylish* boutique hotel I could find for my lovable yet high-maintenance city friends who were adamant about being in the heart of central London. www.therockwell.com

- *The Colonnade Townhouse.* This is the most luxurious and opulent hotel on my list. However, because of its off-the-beaten-path location, the room rates are surprisingly affordable. Situated steps away from the charming canal-side neighborhood of Little Venice, this hotel is only one tube stop from Paddington Station—which makes it ideal for spending time out and about in Central London. Advance booking gets you the best rate. www.theetoncollection.co.uk

›• *Rent a flat.* You'd be amazed at how much cheaper this can be compared to a London hotel. My mother once rented a two-bedroom flat in Sloane Square (arguably the most expensive address in London) for approximately $250 a night. Take a look at the VRBO listings and make sure you ask for the exact postcode (and look it up on a map), before committing to anything, as many of these flats claim to be in better neighborhoods than they really are. www.vrbo.com/vacation-rentals/europe/england/london

When in doubt, check out ratings on Trip Advisor and look for last-minute luxury bargains on Mr. and Mrs. Smith, www.mrandmrssmith.com/hotel-search.

Looking for something even more regal? Try the Stafford Hotel (Prince Harry is known to have clandestine drinks here) or the Goring Hotel (where the entire Middleton family stayed during Kate's wedding to Prince William)—both are minutes from Buckingham Palace. www.kempinski.com/en/london/the-stafford-london/welcome; www.thegoring.com

# Television

The British Broadcasting Company (BBC) is kind of like the UK equivalent of PBS. You will find absolutely no commercials on BBC TV or radio, but unlike PBS which is funded almost entirely by donations, the BBC is funded almost entirely by the taxpayers. For this reason, every person in the UK who owns a television set is required by law to pay for an annual TV license. That's correct—you must be licensed to drive a car, but you also must be licensed to watch television. They actually do random house checks on people to see if you are watching TV without one—so be sure to pay for yours asap. www.tvlicensing.co.uk

English TV is weird. The commercials (or "adverts") are few and far between compared to the US, but they are so subtle, sophisticated, and nuanced, you often aren't sure what they are trying to sell you. Shows about cooking, gardening, and decorating (stuff that is considered daytime TV in America) actually make up the majority of prime-time programming in England. After 9 p.m., full frontal nudity and bad language is completely allowed. Whereas American soap operas are about rich, beautiful people and the terrible things that happen to them, English soap operas (also shown during prime time) are about poor, ugly people and the terrible things that happen to them. Nevertheless, while you may never get to watch *The Bachelor*, every now and then, the Brits will produce a television series that is absolutely phenomenal. These include:

- *Fawlty Towers*
- *Absolutely Fabulous*
- *The Office*
- *Downton Abbey*

For a vital (and highly entertaining) slice of English culture, I implore you to view the boxed sets of all of the above.

# Radio

BBC Radio is the UK version of NPR. But again, unlike NPR, which is funded almost entirely by donations, BBC Radio is funded almost entirely by the taxpayers.

- *BBC World* is the BBC's international news and current affairs station and boosts the largest audience of any radio news station in the world.

- *BBC Radio 4* is a domestic talk radio station that broadcasts a wide variety of incredibly witty, eloquent, and intellectual programs, including news, comedy, science, and history. My favorite thing about Radio 4 is *Woman's Hour* (weekdays at 10 a.m.). First broadcast in 1947, *Woman's Hour* is forty-five wonderful minutes of reports, interviews, and debates designed specifically to be of interest to British women. I love it because there is always something amusingly English, like "The History of the Dressing Table." www.bbc.co.uk/radio4/features/womans-hour

# Politics

In the US, we have Democrats and Republicans. In the UK, you have the Labour Party and the Conservative Party (also called the Tory Party) and a smaller third party called the Liberal Democrats. (Please note that a UK Republican is a person who is against the monarchy.)

However, the most conservative members of the Tory Party are still considered to be more liberal that most US Democrats.

The majority of UK politicians, regardless of left/right party affili-
ation, are pro-choice, pro–gay rights, pro–stem cell research, and
against any kind of gun legalization. (The running joke is that a
British policeman must shout, "Stop! Or I shall say 'stop' again!")
It is also extremely rare for God or religion to be mentioned in
any kind of political debate. Major UK issues tend to be purely
economical rather than moral—they debate and protest and complain about taxes and pensions, tuition fees and interest rates. So
boring—but *so* much more civilized.

Most government offices are located within the Palace of
Westminster—a historic royal palace and former residence of
kings. The layout of the palace is intricate, with its existing build-
ings containing more than two miles of passages. And within this
beautiful, ancient maze of a building, you will find twenty-three
official bars. By law, the bars must stay open as long as the House
is in session. So while the MPs and their staff sit around waiting
for the voting bells to ring, they drink. Vote. Drink. Vote. Drink.
Vote. Drink. It's no wonder the government runs like such a finely
oiled machine.

You'll find no one violently protesting about unborn children,
demanding the right to own semiautomatic weapons, or insisting
that gay humans are somehow less deserving than straight ones.
No one complains about the topless women that appear every day
in the tabloid newspapers or about the full frontal nudity that appears on most TV stations after 9 p.m. On the surface, England
appears to be an oasis of sheer calm and civilization under the
watchful eye of Her Majesty the Queen.

But tensions are bubbling beneath the surface—Brits are upset
about budget cuts and banking bonuses, about burkas and bike
theft, about Afghanistan and Iraq, about civil liberties and CCTV
cameras, and about the increasing gap between the rich and the

poor. The difference is that they debate these issues in a much more subtle, much more cerebral way.

My English husband once made a joke about George W. Bush in front of two Texans and was nearly punched in the face. Mark my words: you will not find any Englishmen punching anyone over the likes of Thatcher, Blair, Brown, and Cameron. Brits do care about political issues—but as a general rule they don't get emotionally worked up about them.

## Newspapers

While the US has one neutral national newspaper (*USA Today*); the UK has *twelve*, and unlike American journalism, all are unabashedly political, making it clear what policies and politicians they do and don't support—which sometimes makes it difficult to distinguish fact from opinion.

- "*Broadsheets*" are considered more intellectual—these include *The Times, The Telegraph, The Financial Times, The Guardian, The Observer*, and *The Independent*.

- "*Red Tops*" are more populist and celebrity-focused, and along with the news, they kindly publish a full-page photo of a topless girl on page three every single morning. It is not uncommon to sit next to a businessman on the tube who is ogling his daily dose of breasts without an ounce of embarrassment. (Personally, I love to read the Page 3 Girl's hobbies—they usually include something riveting like putting up shelves.) Red Tops include *The Sun, The Star, The Mirror, The Sunday Sport*, and the recently defunct *News of the World*.

🎐 Newspapers that fall somewhere in between are the *Daily Mail* (best paper for the latest royal gossip) and the *Daily Express*.

🎐 Free newspapers are available to London commuters both in the morning (the *Metro*) and evening (the *Evening Standard*).

I find the *Financial Times* and the *Guardian* to have the best journalism, but *The Sunday Times* and *The Evening Standard* offer the best fashion and lifestyle magazines.

# The National Health Service

I could write an entire book on this alone—equal parts fairy tale and horror story.

The British people pay a lot of tax and a huge portion of this tax goes toward providing free health care to every single person living in their country. As an American who has lived in the UK since college, I've not had to pay for health insurance even once in my adult life. It's amazing, really.*

The beauty of the NHS is that it tries to be all things to all people—whether you have a cold, a broken leg, or a brain tumor, have been diagnosed with bulimia, emphysema, or schizophrenia—they are there to help you. (I can't tell you how many of my fellow American grad students were overjoyed to discover that they were

---

* However, please keep in mind that you are only covered for health care while you are physically in the UK—if you travel anywhere else—including back home to the US, you must purchase "travel insurance" to cover any unexpected medical expenses while you are away. Nobody told me this until I'd been living in the UK for nearly three years, so I'm telling you now.

eligible for *free therapy* on the NHS. Not to mention free birth control.) And because it's free, no one in England ever has to choose between their health and their house payments—where I'm afraid this is not always the case in the US.

Despite the fact it is the third largest employer on the planet (right behind the Chinese Army and the Indian railroad), the downfall of the NHS is that it does not have the capacity to be all things to all people—and so while all services are provided, the quality of these services is often diluted.

Don't expect sparkling clean doctor's offices with plush waiting rooms, marble floors, drinking fountains, and potted plants. Most GP (general practitioner) offices are cramped into old London houses with higgledy-piggledy staircases and interiors that have not been painted since the 1950s, so they are almost always a depressingly chipped mint green. You will probably have to hop over a dot matrix printer and a garbage can to get onto the examining table, your nurse will be wearing sweatpants (and her hair won't be tied back), and you will no doubt see hundreds of dirty fingerprints and/or smeared blood somewhere on the wall before you leave. But the doctors *are* competent and the service *is* free, so if you want American-style glamour and gloss—you'll have to go private.

But be warned: Going private means paying a fortune. For example, if you have a baby with the NHS—the entire delivery is free as well as all pre-natal and post-natal care. If you have a baby privately—expect to pay nearly $17,000 per night in the hospital. Many US (and occasionally UK) companies offer private health insurance to their London employees, so make sure to look into what you may be eligible for.

FYI: To say you weren't at work because you were "sick" literally means that you were vomiting. Instead, say you were "ill."

To find and register with your nearest GP, go to: www .myhealth.london.nhs.uk (don't wait until you are ill!).

If you are ill, and can't get a GP appointment, you can find a walk-in center here: www.nhs.uk

# Dentistry

Historically, the one health service that the NHS did *not* cover was dentistry. And this is the number one reason why so many Brits have such terrible teeth. Most British people are so deeply appalled by the very idea of paying for *anything* health-related that they simply opt to neglect their teeth entirely. Nowadays, if you are a severe case, you can become eligible for free dental care on the NHS—but for the most part it remains the one health service in the country that you actually have to pay for.

When I make an appointment for a cleaning in the UK (which generally costs about $50), the dentists usually stare at me blankly.

"But what is the problem?" they ask me.

"No problem," I say. "*Just* a cleaning."

They are usually incredibly puzzled by this because most Brits don't go to the dentist just for a cleaning; they only go if the pain in their mouth has become so severe that they can no longer eat. When UK dentists peer into my mouth and see that I have never had a single cavity, they practically short-circuit.

# Work/Life Balance

My British husband and I are both huge fans of the ingenious TV comedy *The Office*—both the UK and US versions. After watching a few American episodes the other day, my husband said, "You know—despite all the time-wasting that goes on in both offices, I still get the distinct impression that the US employees are doing *more work*."

(Listen—he said it, not me.)

A few small points:

- The British work ethic can't begin to compare with that of the US. Brits actually take tea breaks (more accurately, they feel they are *entitled* to take tea breaks).

- The maternity leave is phenomenal; women have the right to twenty-six paid weeks of maternity leave plus an additional twenty-six weeks of unpaid maternity leave—so *a year* in total.

- By law, UK employees are entitled to a *minimum* of 5.6 weeks of *paid* vacation per year. As a result, some of the poorest and most uneducated people in the country have seen more of the world than most middle-class Americans.

My husband is always saying to me, "So where should we go next month?"—and my first reaction is, "But we *just* went somewhere!" After fifteen years in the UK, my American brain *still* can't get used to the idea of going on vacation every eight weeks. (But the beauty of having such a high cost of living in London means you can travel almost anywhere else in the world and it seems cheap.)

# Patriotism

Whether it be a high school basketball game or 4th of July fireworks, Americans almost always become teary-eyed as we belt out our national anthem. This type of passionate patriotism is par for the course for Americans—even if we hate our government, we *genuinely* love our country and relish those moments when we can immerse ourselves, however briefly, in the loving arms of our national consciousness. The Brits have nothing of the sort. Only during the Queen's Jubilee celebrations and the few hours during which Prince William's wedding to Catherine Middleton was televised—did I witness English people enjoying the same level of joyful, idealistic patriotism that Americans experience on a weekly if not daily basis.

While Americans are a naturally proud bunch of people (we work hard for our achievements and take pleasure in sharing them), the Brits often see displays of pride to be boastful or vain. The same applies to patriotism—they can't be proud of their country because they see that as being proud of themselves—an entirely foreign concept to a nation that prefers self-deprecation. In my opinion, this is precisely why the monarchy thrives; the English can displace feelings of loyalty and love away from themselves and onto their beloved Queen.

Their national anthem is not about them, it's about *her*! And they like it that way. Although they don't exactly sing the rafters down, their solemn mumbling of those ancient, tuneless lyrics is the British way of showing that they are fiercely devoted to their sovereign and the country she represents. If you want to blend in to your adopted country, it can't hurt to learn the words. You might even show them how it's done and shed a tear or two.

## "God Save the Queen" (or King When Applicable)

The authorship of the song is unknown, and since its first publication, different verses have been added and subtracted. Even today, different publications contain different verses in various orders—but the first and third verses are consistent, and they are usually the only ones that are sung:

*God save our gracious Queen,*
*Long live our noble Queen,*
*God save the Queen!*
*Send her victorious,*
*Happy and glorious,*
*Long to reign over us,*
*God save the Queen!*

*O Lord, our God, arise,*
*Scatter her enemies,*
*And make them fall.*
*Confound their politics,*
*Frustrate their knavish tricks,*
*On Thee our hopes we fix,*
*God save us all.*

*Thy choicest gifts in store*
*On her be pleased to pour*
*Long may she reign!*
*May she defend our laws,*
*And ever give us cause,*
*To sing with heart and voice,*
*God save the Queen!*

*Not in this land alone,*
*But be God's mercies known,*
*From shore to shore!*
*Lord make the nations see,*
*That men should brothers be,*
*And form one family,*
*The wide world over.*

*From every latent foe,*
*From the assassin's blow,*
*God save the Queen!*
*O'er her thine arm extend,*
*For Britain's sake defend,*
*Our mother, prince, and friend,*
*God save the Queen!*

## RECOMMENDED READING:

### *The Anglo Files* by Sarah Lyall

Having lived in England for more than a decade as the London correspondent for the *New York Times*, the author has compiled some hilarious observations about Britain and its eccentric inhabitants—including the politicians who behave like drunken frat boys and the Brits who will happily extract their own teeth yet refuse to rinse soap off their dishes.

### *Bring Home the Revolution* by Jonathan Freedland

This British author loves America; he loves our contagious can-do spirit; our determination to take control of our lives, shape our communities, and unabashedly assert what we believe to be our god-given right to life, liberty, and happiness. In fact, he argues that it's high time Britain became more like America! This book is hugely readable and is a welcome reminder of how much I love the country of my birth—and how no matter how quirky and charming the English can be, no matter how much I feel I can learn from their incredible history and culture, there is also a great deal of wisdom that the Brits can learn from us.

*I am American bred,*
*I have seen much to hate here, much to forgive*
*But in a world where England is finished and dead,*
*I do not wish to live.*

—FROM *THE WHITE CLIFFS* BY ALICE DUER MILLER

I have no doubt that people will continue to rant on and on about how girls like you and me should get our Anglophile heads out of the clouds and start living in "the real world." But I honestly think "the real world" is just a phrase that's batted around to give credibility to the miserable lives most people have created for themselves.

At the end of the day, it's pretty simple: You can have the English life that you want *or* you can have everyone else's reasons for not having it . . .

## Confronting Your Critics

I'm sure everyone you encounter thinks your London-bound plan is ludicrous. I'm sure they think it's expensive, unnecessary, and downright silly—and I'm sure they have no problem telling you so. But one way that dreams can become suppressed is when we are made to feel as if we are the only ones in the world crazy enough to even have dreams. But you know what? Those grumpy people who refuse to support you in manifesting your dreams of English happiness are doing nothing but delaying their own unique dreams from coming true.

I'm sure some of the naysayers in your life are absolutely right— you *do* have the potential to do all sorts of *other* amazing things that don't involve crossing an ocean and settling down in a foreign country. But you don't have to do those things just because they're expected of you, or because others tell you that you should do them, or because you'd be incredibly good at them. All that following your head instead of your heart nonsense is highly overrated. Despite all your attempts to ignore it or to pretend that you can't hear what the little voice inside your heart is saying, you'll never be able to keep it quiet. It will always be there, forever repeating to you that England is where you must go. You owe it to yourself to listen.

Looking back, I had no idea what I was doing when I moved to London—but even so, I made sure to do it as hard as I possibly could. So my advice to you is this: Know what you want, know that you deserve it, and believe that you can get it. (And always remember that getting there isn't half the fun—sometimes it's *all* the fun!)

Try to ignore what everyone else is saying and keep a death grip on your dream. Don't give up gracefully or leave England at the very first obstacle—stand your ground. Decide to abandon your dream only if you are dragged away from it kicking and screaming. And while some people will say how dare you go after your dream—rest assured that others will silently be thanking you for showing them how.

# The American Dream

"But you're *American*," some people tell me pointedly (almost as if I didn't know). "Don't you think you belong in your own country?"

I've never understood this question. I mean, let's be honest: Where would America be today if two hundred years ago, everyone in the world had stayed in their own countries?

Living in another country does not make you anti-American, nor does it make you unpatriotic. Living in another country actually means that you have *embraced* the American dream to the fullest! You have taken advantage of the freedom and opportunity at your fingertips and set out to do what you always dreamed of. No matter where you came from, who your family is, or how much money you may or may not have—you *knew* that if you worked hard and had faith in yourself you could achieve your heart's desire. That unwavering desire just happens to be in England. But the path that put you there? *That* is the American dream in its purest form.

I am a staunch royalist, a proud Anglophile, and this winter will acquire the UK passport I've longed for my whole life. However, not for a single second have I forgotten than none of this would be possible without the very American belief that we can do anything we set our minds to.

(Luckily, both America and the UK allow dual citizenship.)

# Self-Belief

*No one can make you feel inferior without your consent.*
—ELEANOR ROOSEVELT

Despite all the airs and graces, deep down, Brits are quite vulnerable (which is perhaps why they rely so much on giant hats to protect them). While expats should always make an effort to fit into their adopted country (partly out of respect and partly for self-preservation), keep in mind that there are so many complicated and nuanced layers to English society and culture that "being English" is a club that quite often not even the English can get into!

I am still noticeably American—I speak more softly than most of my countrymen, and I use UK terms instead of US ones, but my accent is pure Western Colorado. I may be wearing English tweed and Scottish cashmere, but my grooming and dental habits are 100 percent American. My knowledge of etiquette and table manners is entirely English, but my cheery enthusiasm and starry-eyed optimism were clearly born in the USA.

So even if you're surrounded by British people who have been inducted since birth in the rituals of their world, who grew up knowing and caring about things like hereditary titles and family crests, what really matters is your belief that you are perfectly entitled to stand among them. England is indeed a fairy-tale kingdom, but you must know that it is one you are worthy of and one that you deserve to enjoy. Above all, you must have confidence and believe in yourself. Always remember that if you carry yourself with dignity and grace, then you have every right to move in regal circles.

And move in them you will.

Required (as opposed to recommended) Reading:

*Someday My Prince Will Come: True Adventures of a Wannabe Princess* by Jerramy Fine

Most young girls dream of becoming a princess, but unlike most girls, Jerramy Fine (yep—that's me!) never grew out of it. At age six, she announces she is going to meet and marry the Queen of England's grandson, and even as she gets older, not once does she change her mind! But growing up with hippie parents in the middle of a Colorado farm town makes finding her prince a bigger challenge than Jerramy ever bargained for. How can she prepare to lead a royal life when she's surrounded by nothing but tofu and tractors?

Jerramy spends her lonely childhood writing love letters to Buckingham Palace, and when her sense of destiny finally brings her to London, she dives headfirst into a whirlwind of society parties in search of her royal soul mate. She drinks way too many martinis and kisses far too many Hugh Grant look-alikes, but life in England is not the Disney fairy tale she hoped it would be. Her flatmates are lunatics, London is expensive, and British boys (despite their cute accents) are infuriating. Sure, she's rubbing shoulders with Princess Anne, Earl Spencer, and the Duchess of York—but will she ever meet her prince?

*Someday My Prince Will Come* is a hilarious *true* story about following your heart and having the courage to pursue your childhood dream no matter how impossible it seems.

(And I promise you this: if *I* could do it—you can too.)

## SPECIAL THANKS

To Olivia Smales, Olivia Vandyk, Jane Finette, Elizabeth Kinder, Julie Collins-Clark, and (my protégée) Courtney Fleming—not only for your stellar proofreading, but for your friendship, and in many cases, anecdotal inspiration. I owe you a Mahiki treasure chest.

To my agent, Laura Langlie, and my editor, Kate Seaver—for not only "getting" my drastic case of Anglophilia, but championing it.

To my long-suffering English husband—for indulging my insatiable obsession with his country and its customs, and for teaching me that some US-UK relationships are more special than I ever imagined.

To my long-suffering American parents—who never once discouraged me from spreading my wings, fleeing the nest, and flying alone across the sun.

# PHOTO AND IMAGE CREDITS